BARRON'S

HOW TO PREPARE FOR THE

U.S. CITIZENSHIP TEST

6TH EDITION

BARRON'S

HOW TO PREPARE FOR THE
U.S. CITIZENSHIP TEST

6TH EDITION

Gladys E. Alesi, M.B.A.

Executive Director
American Immigration and Citizenship Conference

Former Consultant to the
Department of Justice,
Immigration and Naturalization Service

Former Administrator of English and
Citizenship Program of
New York City Board of Education

BARRON'S

All inquiries should be addressed to:
Barron's Educational Series, Inc.
250 Wireless Boulevard
Hauppauge, New York 11788
http://www.barronseduc.com

Library of Congress Catalog Card No. 2004055077
ISBN-13: 978-0-7641-2379-5
ISBN-10: 0-7641-2379-3

Library of Congress Cataloging-in-Publication Data

Alesi, Gladys E.
    Barron's How to prepare for the U.S. citizenship test / Gladys Alesi.—6th ed.
        p. cm.
    Rev. ed. of: How to prepare for the U.S. citizenship test. 5th ed. c2000.
    Includes index.
    ISBN 0-7641-2379-3 (alk. paper)
    1. Citizenship—United States—Examinations, questions, etc. 2. Citizenship—
United States—Examinations—Study guides. I. Title: How to prepare for the
U.S. citizenship test. II. Title: U.S. citizenship test. III. Alesi, Gladys E.
How to prepare for the U.S. citizenship test. IV. Title.

JK1758.A614   2005
323.6'23'0973—dc22

                                                                    2004055077

Printed in the United States of America
9 8 7 6 5 4

Contents

LIST OF CHARTS AND ILLUSTRATIONS

Introduction

This is a complete road map to American citizenship by way of naturalization. It contains comprehensive, easy-to-read instructions for the legally admitted aliens who want to become citizens, in accordance with the latest laws and regulations.

To reach the point of readiness for naturalization, the book includes many practice exercises and pretests needed to develop language skills and the knowledge of American history and government needed for the interview. It contains sample questions like those asked by the naturalization examiner at the time of the interview. It contains some of the forms required, as well as information on how to obtain others that may be needed by some applicants.

What it does *not* contain is legal advice for applicants with special legal problems. Those with questions about eligibility, entry, status, etc., should seek professional help before they file. Professional help is available from private immigration attorneys. Ask a citizen, who has consulted one, or check the Yellow Pages of the local telephone book. Those who need legal help, but cannot afford to hire an immigration attorney, are advised to check with community agencies for accredited free service. Field offices of U.S. Citizenship and Immigration Services (USCIS) contain some information on these agencies.

How to Prepare for the U.S. Citizenship Test is a guide to becoming an American citizen that works for all who follow the steps to citizenship. The writing exercises are adapted from sentences dictated by an interviewer. The reading exercises and questions on American civics and government are samples of the ones asked by the USCIS officer at the interview. In addition, the book provides a ready reference on the background of American history and culture, through Meet the Presidents (page 134) and American holidays (page 115).

All of the preparation materials in this book are in accordance with present immigration law. At this time (2004), changes are being contemplated by the United States Congress. Because changes are possible, it is important to check with the USCIS office for the most current information. If you are affected by these changes, it is best to consult an immigration attorney.

A Letter from the Author

Welcome,

You already have a green card; you are 18 years of age or over; you have entered the country legally. Now you are ready to go on. Welcome to "A Nation of Immigrants," joining others who believe in freedom and justice. It is time for you to participate in your new country as an American citizen!

You do that by naturalization, which this book tells you all about. For now, this book tells you that, "The highest law of our land is the Constitution. It defines the rights and duties of a citizen. The Constitution states that a person born or naturalized in the United States is a citizen of the United States and of the State where he resides."

A citizen has many rights and privileges. A naturalized citizen has all the rights of a native-born citizen except for one, and that is, a naturalized citizen can never become President of the United States—every other job may be a possibility! A naturalized citizen has responsibilities, too. They include loyalty to the United States, its Constitution, and its laws.

Naturalization is the way to go if you have decided to become an American citizen! I have taught immigrants for many years, and have friends who went from alien to citizen as soon as they could. Now they have all the rights and responsibilities of American citizens, just like I do.

At the last naturalization hearing I went to, one of my new friends said, "Life is what you make it. You can make it good in the United States of America!" This book will help you if you follow the steps.

Sincerely,

Gladys Alesi

Gladys Alesi

Acknowledgments

I gratefully acknowledge the kindness of those concerned with granting permission to reprint passages, charts, and drawings. Special appreciation is offered to the U.S. Department of Justice, whose descriptive drawings, charts, and sample test (which has been expanded and adapted) have helped to enhance this publication. Without the help of my daughter, Catherine A. McCollum, I could never have brought this guide to conclusion. Her unfailing empathy and support combined with her research assistance made this edition possible.

How to Use This Book

This is a workbook. That means you must work all the exercises in the order they are presented. You must follow the instructions if you want to succeed.

READ 1 TO 6 aloud to a friend or in front of a mirror.

1. I am at least 18 years old. I am _____ years old.
2. I was legally admitted for permanent residence, or I applied for legalization, according to the Immigration and Control Act.
3. I have resided here for at least five years, unless I qualify for an exception (see page 19).
4. I am a person of good moral character.
5. I am willing to take an Oath of Allegiance to the United States of America.
6. That is just the beginning. I am learning to speak, read, and write English. I am learning about the history and government of my new country.

When you are alone, practice saying the above as many times as you can!

Now, read this—

This book has two parts:

PART ONE—called FIRST STEPS

Take the Pretest. Check your answers. If you passed the test you are ready to go on. If you failed the test, do all the reading exercises. Put a line under a word you do not understand, and look it up in the Reference Section of the book.

Take the Pretest again. Check your answers. Continue taking the test until you pass.

PART TWO—called FINAL STEPS

Obtain the application form (N-400). Practice filling in the blanks on the form, in pencil. Check the instructions.

File your application, with fees and everything needed, and WAIT.

In the meantime, practice for the interview, do all of the reading and writing exercises, check the Probability Questions and the answers.

Appear for the interview at the time and place you are told. Answer every question slowly and thoughtfully.

Take the Oath of Allegiance.

Each part is explained in great detail in this book. Check the Contents now.

Did You Understand?

Did you understand all of that? This is a repetition of the last page. The more you repeat, the better you learn.

Now, read this:

This book is in two parts. Part One contains two steps. Part Two contains six steps. Here is a short summary of each step:

PART ONE—FIRST STEPS

Step 1: A pretest to show you where you are right now. If you do well on this test, you are ready to start filing your application. If you do not do well, do all the reading exercises in Part One before you go on to Part Two.

Step 2: Reading exercises to give you practice in using citizenship words and ideas.

PART TWO—FINAL STEPS

Step 1: Obtain the forms and check the fees. You may have some questions.

Step 2: File your application. Make sure you send in the correct fee and the documents required.

Step 3: Reading and writing exercises to improve your English language skills.

Step 4: Reading exercises to improve your knowledge of history and civics (government).

Step 5: Probability Questions to prepare for the interview.

Step 6: Take the Oath of Allegiance.

Quiz

Read these questions and write the answers on the lines.

1. How many parts are in this book? _____

2. What is a pretest? _____

   _____

3. Which section will help you with written English? _____

   _____

4. Which section will tell about our government and history? _____

   _____

5. Which section will tell you about the interview? _____

   _____

Check your answers before going on to Part One.
(Turn the book upside down to find the correct answers.)

Read About Tests

There are many tests in this book. They provide the practice you need. Another word for test is *quiz*. Some of the short tests are called *reviews*. A review means "a systematic study of something just learned." Halfway through this book, you will find *progress tests*. Take all of them, even those that seem difficult at first. You will gain confidence as you do them again and again. Look ahead to the time you can discuss them as a citizen!

Now go to Part One. Take a very important test—the Pretest. Read it first. Then write the answers. Go to page 3, now.

5. Step 5
4. Step 4
3. Part Two, Step 3
2. A test given before instruction
1. Two

ANSWERS

xii

PART ONE—
★★★★★★★★★★★★★★★★★★★★★★★★
First Steps

Take the Pretest

Do this.

Read the questions aloud. Do not write.

The first five questions are all about you. Read the questions again and print the answers. Check them carefully.

1. What is your family name? (last name) _____

   _____

2. What is your given name? (first name) _____

   _____

3. Where do you live now? (city/state) _____

   _____

4. Where were you born? _____

   _____

5. When were you born? (month/day/year) _____

   _____

Questions 6 to 15 are about the United States. Read the questions aloud. The answers to the questions are here. Choose the correct answer and print it in the space.

50	Congress	President
blue	governor	Constitution
vote	democracy	executive, legislative, judicial
republic		Supreme Court

Check your answers with the answers at the bottom of the page.

6. The American flag is red, white, and _____

7. How many states are in the United States? _____

_____

8. What form of government does the United States have? _____

_____

9. Who makes the laws for the country? _____

_____

10. What are the three branches of the government? _____

_____

11. What is the supreme law of the land? _____

_____

12. What is the highest court in the United States? _____

_____

13. What is the title of the chief executive of the United States government? _____

_____

14. What is the title of the chief executive of the state government? __

_____

15. What can a citizen do that an alien cannot? _____

_____

How many did you answer correctly? _____
If you answered 7 of the 10 questions correctly, you are ready to take the next step.

Looking Ahead

The Pretest showed you some of the things you need to know. You also need to improve your English language skills. You can do this at the same time as you learn about the government and history of your new country, that is, if you follow all the instructions. You will be given reviews so that you are well prepared when the time comes for you to take the Oath of Allegiance to your new country!

Think what it will be like when you have your citizenship papers! Or, when you ask a neighbor, for the first time, "Where do I go to vote?" You can look forward to that if you follow the steps to citizenship in this book. You can do it! It may seem long and difficult but time passes quickly when you take the steps.

Practice makes perfect! That old saying tells you how to do it. Reading and answering questions about what you have read will help. Get a local newspaper to read, and try to make up your own questions about what you have read. Put a line under words you don't understand. Find out what they mean by asking a neighbor, by looking up the word in the Word List at the back of this book, or by using a dictionary. Most important, take all of the tests in this section. Whenever you can, read them out loud. Do each exercise several times. Follow the instructions each step of the way.

Now, turn the page and read about the American flag. Answer the questions about it. You may hear a question about the flag at your naturalization examination. You are looking ahead to American citizenship—it takes time and work. Take the first step.

The Flag

Another word for flag is *banner*. The national anthem is the "Star-Spangled Banner." Sometimes the flag is called Old Glory.

Now read this poem about the flag and answer the questions about it.

America Is Her Flag

Fifty stars are in her flag
for the 50 states in her Union.
June 14, 1777, the flag of the United States of America
had 13 stars—one for each state in the new Union.

This flag had 13 stripes,
a ribbon for each of the first colonies.

And poets say the colors in our flag
stand for the things we hold dear—
red for courage,
white for truth,
blue for honor.

A country is as strong as its ideals.

We love the things for which Old Glory stands.

You can help hold these colors high.

Figure 1

Source: *U.S. Department of Justice, Immigration and Naturalization Service*

1. What are the colors of the American flag? _____

   _____

2. What do the colors stand for? _____

   _____

3. How many stripes are in the flag? _____

   _____

4. How many stars are in the flag? _____

   _____

5. What is the national anthem (song)? _____

   _____

Now check your answers. The answers to these questions are on page 169.

Reading Practice Exercises

You have read some general information about citizenship in the United States. Now you will again read some of the same information, broken down into exercises for reading comprehension.

There are six reading exercises and a summary. Do them in order—the first, second, and so on—answering the questions before you go to the next passage. Check your answers with those on pages 169–173. Do not give up until they are all correct!

Now, begin with reading exercise 1. Follow instructions. Read out loud so you will become familiar with the sounds of English.

1. What Citizenship Means

Do you know what a citizen is? A **citizen** is a part of his or her country. In the United States, a citizen is a free man or woman—free to make choices and free to help pick the people who govern. The opposite of a citizen is an **alien,** or stranger. You want to become a citizen! A person who likes the business he or she works for may want to become a partner, but it is not always easy to become a partner in a business. The United States government, however, makes it easy for you to become a partner in *its* business.

A citizen has many rights. The most important one is the right to vote. A citizen can vote in national, state, and local elections. A citizen helps to decide who will be president of the United States and who will make the laws for the nation, state, and city. A citizen can also vote for the local school board, the group of men and women who decide on the policies for the public schools.

There are other rights. For example, certain jobs are open only to citizens. These are often civil service jobs that offer security and many benefits. There is no question of a citizen's legal rights to receive Social Security payments in later life or to obtain welfare, if needed. American citizens with American passports are free to travel all over the world. Citizens do not have to report changes of address to the attorney general within 10 days of occurrence, as aliens must.

To sum up, a citizen belongs. But nothing in life comes free. There are costs to be shared. Yes, there is a price, but the price is right! You will learn what that price is.

REVIEW

Do you know what these words mean? Write the meaning next to each word. If you are not sure, look up the meaning in the Word List at the end of this book.

1. alien _____

2. citizen _____

3. democracy _____

4. security _____

5. benefit _____

Now read the following questions. Write the answers in the spaces provided.

6. The opposite of *right* is *wrong*.

   a. What is the opposite of *citizen?* _____

   _____

   b. What is the opposite of *difficult?* _____

   _____

7. Is it easy or difficult to become a citizen? _____

   _____

8. Do you want to be a citizen or an alien? _____

   _____

9. What are some of the benefits of citizenship? _____

   _____

   _____

10. What are some of the rights of a citizen that you want to have?___

   _____

   _____

Check your answers with the answer key on page 169.

2. What Naturalization Means

Naturalization includes the word *natural* and it means giving an alien (or foreign-born person) the rights and privileges of a natural-born citizen.

Naturalization means taking certain steps set by law to become a citizen. These steps are petitioning or asking for citizenship, proving eligibility and residence here, and taking the Oath of Allegiance (a promise of loyalty) to the United States of America.

Look at the people you meet on the job, in your neighborhood, at school, and in government offices. Most of them are citizens. Some of them were born here; others were **naturalized.** These others came here as strangers or immigrants and became citizens by naturalization.

Immigrants are people who enter the country for the purpose of living here. We are a nation of immigrants, as President John F. Kennedy told us in his book of that title. He said that the first settlers who came to this country in the 16th century and those who come today, wanting to live here, are all immigrants or the children of immigrants!

Another president, George H. W. Bush, said that America's greatness was "forged (created) by the talents, the hard work, and the hopes of people who came to our shores." He said that at a naturalization ceremony on Citizenship Day, September 17, 1988, before he became president.

"Welcome, new Americans," those are the words that open the naturalization ceremony. You will also hear those words when you are sworn in. You may also hear something like this: "Be proud of your roots, love the places where you have lived, and be proud of your success in attaining citizenship!"

Recent immigrants have had help from the Immigration Reform and Control Act of 1986, the Immigration Act of 1990, and the Nicaraguan and Central American Relief Act. Among them have been refugees, people who can never go home again. They benefited from the Refugee Act of 1980. This law allowed people who were persecuted, or who have a well-founded fear of persecution on account of race, religion, national origin, or political opinion, or membership in a particular social group to reside in the United States of America.

All of these people are welcomed here. They go through the same steps to naturalization as you will. And you will become a citizen as earlier immigrants did, with the important rights of a natural-born American citizen!

Let us look at the last step in the naturalization process. You are in a large courtroom in front of a judge. Perhaps, as in a big city, there are many other people there, too. Some of your friends and relatives may be there, sitting on the benches behind you.

The clerk of the court says the words of the Oath of Allegiance. You repeat the words. In brief, they say that you will be loyal to the Constitution and laws of the United States of America. That is what you swear to do.

Other people who by law must take oaths like this one are the president and vice president, as well as many high government officials. The oath ends with the words, *So help me, God!*

After taking this oath, you are an American citizen. You will receive your Certificate of Naturalization (citizenship papers). Now, you have all the benefits of citizenship.

You are not an alien or stranger, but a part of this country! You can vote, run for office, and be elected to all positions except two: the president and vice president of the United States of America.

You have read about the last step in the naturalization process. In Part Two you will go back to the beginning and find out what the first step is. But first, do the review exercise on this page. And read passages 3, 4, 5, 6, and 7.

REVIEW

Do you know what these words mean? Write the meaning next to each word. If you are not sure, look up the meanings in the Word List at the end of this book.

1. naturalized _____

2. settle _____

3. immigrant _____

4. refugee _____

5. oath _____

6. allegiance _____

7. persecution _____

8. political opinion _____

Now, write the answers to the following questions in the space provided.

9. Where does naturalization take place? _____
_____

10. What is the Oath of Allegiance? _____
_____

11. Why do you want to become a citizen of the United States? _____
_____

12. Can a naturalized citizen become a U.S. Senator, a mayor, a governor? _____
_____

13. Can a naturalized citizen become president of the United States (or vice president)? _____
_____

See the answer key on page 169.

Practice your English by reading the passage below in front of a mirror or have someone listen to your pronunciation. Then answer the questions.

3. Immigration

From earliest times, people have migrated (moved) from one place to another. When the first colonists came to this land in the 1600s, they worked hard to settle and build a great country. Since that time, about 40 million settlers have come and been welcomed here.

Records of immigrants were first kept in 1820. For that year, the number of immigrants was about 8,000. This number grew steadily and by the middle of the 1800s, it increased 10 times. By the end of the century (1899), the first laws against "free immigration" were in effect.

Congress has since made laws to control the number of aliens coming to this country as immigrants. In 1986 the Immigration Reform and Control Act (IRCA) was created to legalize aliens who had lived here, worked here, or who came here to join their families.

A recent law is the Immigration Act of 1990, passed by Congress and signed by President George H. W. Bush as Public Law 101-649. This book is in accord (agreement) with both of these laws. You can read about these laws in the Immigration Update section.

REVIEW

Now write the answers to these questions in the spaces provided.

1. What does migration mean?_____

   _____

2. About how many immigrants have come here from the 1600s to the present? _____

3. What is a recent immigration law?_____

4. When was the first immigration law passed? _____

5. When did the first colonists (settlers) come to this country? _____

   _____

Put a line under the words in the passage that answer each question. If you are not sure, read it again and check your answers before you go on to the next section. At the end of this unit is a summary of steps called How to Move from Alien to Citizen. Read it as you did this reading exercise. Put lines under words that you do not understand. Later, look them up in the Word List.

See the answer key on page 170.

SOME OF OUR FIRST IMMIGRANTS

People from many foreign lands came and settled in this new world. They sought liberty and a better living, and the happiness they hoped these would bring them. Here are some of the early arrivals:

1565	The SPANISH settled at St. Augustine, in what is now Florida.
1607	The ENGLISH settled at Jamestown, in what is now Virginia.
1620	The ENGLISH (Pilgrims) settled in what is now Massachusetts.
1623–1625	The DUTCH settled on Manhattan Island, where New York City has since been built.
1638	The SWEDES settled in what is now the State of Delaware.
1681	The ENGLISH (Quakers) settled in what is now Pennsylvania.
1683	The GERMANS settled at Germantown and other places in Pennsylvania.
1714	The SCOTTISH and IRISH settled in large numbers along the western edge of all the colonies from Pennsylvania to Georgia.
1718	The FRENCH settled in New Orleans, at the mouth of the Mississippi River.

Figure 2

Source: U.S. Department of Justice, Immigration and Naturalization Service

4. Rights of Citizens

The Constitution is the supreme, or highest, law of the United States. It was written a long time ago and became the law of the land for the United States of America in 1789. Since that time, it has been changed, or **amended,** 27 times. This means that there are 27 amendments to the Constitution of the United States of America. The Fourteenth Amendment was adopted in 1868 following the end of slavery in the United States. The amendment states the rights of citizens, as follows:

> *All persons born or naturalized in the United States, and subject to the <u>jurisdiction</u> thereof, are citizens of the United States and of the State <u>wherein they reside.</u> No state shall make or enforce any law which shall <u>abridge</u> the privileges or <u>immunities</u> of citizens of the United States; nor shall any State <u>deprive</u> any person of life, liberty, or property, without due process of law; nor deny to any person within its <u>jurisdiction</u> the equal protection of the laws.*

Here is the same article stated in simple English:

> *All persons born or naturalized in the United States, and living here under U.S. law, are citizens of the United States and of the state in which they live (<u>reside</u>). No state can make or carry out a law that limits (<u>abridges</u>) a citizen's Constitutional privileges or freedom. And no state can take away (<u>deprive</u>) life, liberty, or property without following fixed legal rules and procedures. All citizens are to be treated equally under the law and are entitled to the same protection within each state. Wherever a citizen travels, he or she is protected by the United States of America.*

A citizen has a voice in the government. Only a citizen can vote for the officials who make the rules under which he or she lives, and only a citizen can hold office if elected. A citizen may work for the government under civil service.

REVIEW

Do you know what these words mean? Write the meanings next to the words. If you are not sure, look up the meaning in the Word List at the end of the book.

1. amendment _____

2. jurisdiction _____

3. residence _____

4. abridge _____

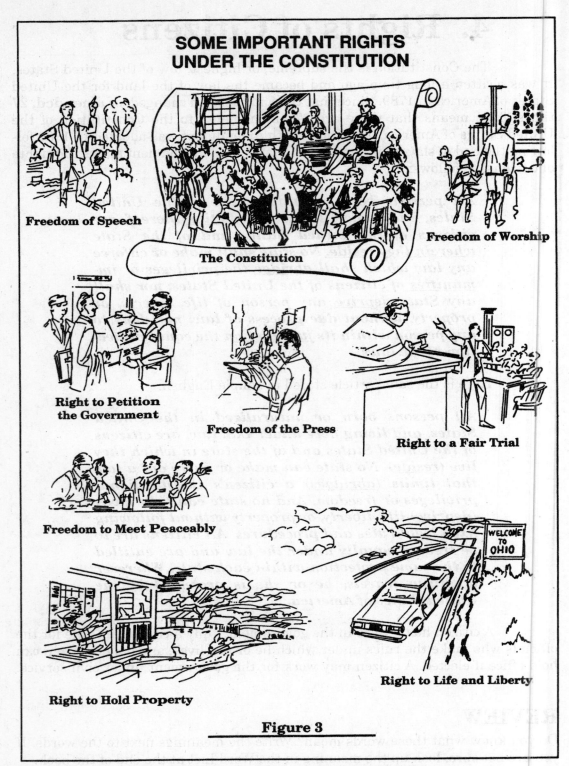

SOME IMPORTANT RIGHTS UNDER THE CONSTITUTION

Freedom of Speech

The Constitution

Freedom of Worship

Right to Petition the Government

Freedom of the Press

Right to a Fair Trial

Freedom to Meet Peaceably

WELCOME TO OHIO

Right to Life and Liberty

Right to Hold Property

Figure 3

Source: U.S. Department of Justice, Immigration and Naturalization Service

5. immunity _____

6. deprive _____

Now write the answers to the following questions in the spaces provided.

7. What is the highest law of the land? _____

_____

8. How many amendments are there? _____

9. Which amendment tells about the rights of citizens? _____

_____

10. Can you tell what these rights are? _____

_____

11. Which of the rights is the most important to you? _____

_____

See the answer key on page 170.

5. Responsibilities of Citizens

Citizenship has many benefits and all citizens must pay for these benefits; the price was right.

There is a Spanish proverb that tells us to "take what we want and pay for it." We have made a choice. We have chosen to become citizens. Now we must pay for that choice. We must register to vote and then vote on Election Day. We must work with others to make this a better place in which to live. Our government is a **democracy.** This means that through our vote we have a voice in government. We also have the right to join a political party. In doing so, we join with others who feel as we do.

Knowing all you can about the issues and keeping up-to-date on what is going on in your country are other responsibilities. The quality of government is improved when voters know who the candidates for office are.

When persons are tried for criminal or civil offenses, they are often judged guilty or innocent by a jury of their peers. This means that people who are citizens have to be willing to give their time to serve on a jury. When you become a citizen, you may be called for jury duty. One of the prices of citizenship is to be willing to serve if you are called. You will not be called more than once a year.

We can say that the price of citizenship includes doing the following:

- Keeping informed about what is going on
- Voting in every election
- Obeying the laws
- Paying taxes
- Defending the country if it becomes necessary*
- Serving on a jury if called
- Being willing to hold office

QUIZ

Do you know what these words mean? Write the meanings next to the words. If you are not sure, look them up in the Word List at the end of the book.

1. benefit _____

2. democracy _____

3. responsibility _____

4. informed _____

5. criminal _____

6. civil _____

7. jury _____

Now write the answers to these questions in the space provided.

8. Are all the benefits of citizenship free? _____

    _____

9. What is the price of citizenship? _____

    _____

10. Why should a citizen vote? _____

11. Why should a citizen serve on a jury? _____

    _____

12. What are the responsibilities of citizenship? _____

    _____

See the answer key on page 170.

_____
*If it is not against your religion to do so.

6. Exceptions to Some Requirements for Naturalization

In reviewing the main requirements for naturalization (see p. x), note that there are some *exceptions*. For example:

Item 2—You must have been legally admitted to the United States for permanent residence. The amnesty law passed in 1986 helps former illegal aliens to establish lawful permanent residence. (See section on Immigration Update.)

Item 3—You must have been a legal resident of the United States continuously for at least five years. Some exceptions to this rule are wives, husbands, or children of citizens, or persons in the armed forces or navy.

Item 4—You must understand English and be able to read, write, and speak ordinary English. One exception to this rule is an applicant who is older than 50 years old and has lived in the United States for at least 20 years.

Item 5—You must have a knowledge and understanding of the history and government of the United States. An applicant who has a physical or developmental disability or a mental impairment may be eligible for an exception to this requirement.

Item 6—You must be prepared to take the Oath of Allegiance to the United States. The USCIS may excuse some applicants from this requirement.

Answer the quiz that follows.

QUIZ

Answer these five questions. Check your answers with the answer key on page 170.

1. Item 1 of the requirements was left out in this passage. Do you remember what it was? _____

2. Is there any exception to that requirement? _____

3. Where is the section on Immigration Update?_____

4. What is one exception to the residence requirement? _____

_____

5. Is there any exception to the requirement that you must take and understand the Oath of Allegiance to the United States?_____

_____

If you meet the main requirements, you are ready to look at the 25 probability questions on page 48. Some of them have been asked at the naturalization interview. These questions are asked in simple everyday English to find out how much the applicant knows about American history and government. As indicated earlier, you should know the names of your two senators and the congressman or congresswoman who represents you.

Write them here again: **SENATOR** _____

SENATOR _____

REPRESENTATIVE (MEMBER OF CONGRESS)

_____

You have read six (6) passages containing words connected with naturalization and citizenship, and you have taken short tests on your reading. Have you done well? Do you feel that you understand what you have read? Let us see about that!

Now read number 7, the summary. See if you can explain, in your own words, about moving from alien to citizen. Practice writing about it, too.

7. Summary: How to Move from Alien to Citizen

Moving from alien to citizen is set by law. Immigration laws are made by the Congress of the United States. Everything in this book concerning the admission of aliens, the legalization of undocumented aliens (persons not admitted as permanent residents), and the unification of families is in accord with the most recent Immigration and Nationality Act, and reflects all laws as of October 2003. A lawfully admitted alien can be naturalized if he or she meets the requirements (see page x).

The law states that "a person may only be naturalized as a citizen of the United States in the manner and under the conditions prescribed, and not otherwise." In this unit you have read what these conditions are. You know that what is prescribed is what must be followed. You can do it, as many before you have done!

As one of our presidents wrote, our country is "a nation of immigrants." If the number of immigrants come in at the current rate of about 800,000 per year, we will continue this way. And some, like you, will aspire to citizenship. As you know, it takes time to become a full American citizen. Those who use their time wisely to prepare themselves will succeed.

This is the end of Part One. Go back to page 3 and take the pretest again.

If you pass, you are ready to go ahead to Part Two.

PART TWO—
★★★★★★★★★★★★★★★★★★★★★★★
Final Steps

Climbing the Steps—An Introduction

Begin here after you pass the Pretest. You are ready! You are on your way. First, read this brief review of the law:

The Immigration and Nationality Act requires you to have an understanding of the English language, history, principles, and form of government of the United States. You must be able to read, write, and speak words in ordinary usage in the English language, UNLESS you are over 50 years old and have resided here for 20 years, or over 55 years old and have resided here for 15 years, or have a physical or developmental disability or a mental impairment. You must have a knowledge of the history, principles, and government of the United States, no matter what your age. The only exception to this requirement is a physical or mental disability. No person may apply who is opposed to our government or law, or who favors totalitarian forms of government.

Who Can Apply?

A lawfully admitted adult, at least 18 years of age, who has resided in the United States for five years or more as a permanent resident, or who has married a United States citizen and has lived with the spouse for three years or more.

All statements in this book are based on the Immigration and Nationality Act, and reflect regulations adopted as of October 1, 2003.

Getting Started

Read this out loud:

I am eligible for naturalization because:

- I am 18 years old or older.
- I was legally admitted for permanent residence, or I applied for legalization under the law.
- I have resided here for at least 5 years, unless I have an exemption.
- I am a person of good moral character.
- I meet the educational requirements, unless I have an exemption.

Did you understand all of that? Now read this:

This is Part Two. It contains five steps for you to follow to get ready for naturalization. They are:

Step 1: How to Begin
            Forms and Fees
            Some Questions You May Have
Step 2: Filing Your Form
            Form N-400: Now Fill Out the Real Thing
            Probability Questions
Step 3: Serious Study—English
            Practice Test of Written English
            Reading Practices I, II, and III
            Review: More Writing Practice
Step 4: Serious Study—History and Civics
            Our Government
            The Constitution
            Reading Practice
            Summary: How The Bill of Rights Protects Americans
            The Federal Government: Form and Structure
            State and Local Governments
            The Declaration of Independence
            The American Flag
            The Final Test
Step 5: The Naturalization Interview
            Review of the Steps to Citizenship
            Review of the Probability Questions
Step 6: Take the Oath

Step 1— How to Begin

Forms and Fees

Get the forms you need to file for naturalization. These forms may be obtained by calling the U.S. Citizenship and Immigration Services (USCIS) at 1-800-870-3676 (free call). You may also obtain the form from the USCIS page on the Internet at http://www.uscis.gov.

Having received the forms that you requested, you now should look them over carefully. Do you understand what information is needed? It may be necessary to find some of your own papers that are referred to. You should also become familiar with other forms that you may need.

If you check the Application for Naturalization, you may find that you also need other forms. The table on page 26 is a list of commonly used forms.

All fees should be paid by check or money order and should be made out to the *United States Citizenship and Immigration Services.*

Following the table of forms and fees is Form N-400. Use this form for practice. Read the instructions carefully. Print the information, using a pencil. Fill out the form completely. Look for the documents you need. Look for them now. If you were ever arrested, no matter for how small an offense, look for the papers on that arrest.

FORM NUMBER	FORM TITLE	FORM FEE*
N-400	Application for Naturalization	$320
N-565	Application for Replacement of Naturalization/Citizenship Certificate	$210
N-600	Application for Certificate of Citizenship	$240
N-600K	Application for Citizenship and Issuance of a Certificate Under Section 322	##
N-648	Medical Certification for Disability Exceptions	None
I-90	Application to Replace Permanent Resident Card	$185
I-130	Petition for Alien Relative	$185
I-485	Application to Register Permanent Residence or Adjust Status	$315

$240 for an application filed on behalf of a biological child.
$200 for an application filed on behalf of an adopted child.

*As of April 30, 2004   Fees DO NOT include the $70 service fee for fingerprinting.

WARNING: People (or Internet Web sites) may offer you USCIS forms if you pay a fee. These forms may be out of date. Using them could slow down your application. Up-to-date USCIS forms are available for free from the USCIS Internet site, http://uscis.gov.

People (or Internet Web sites) may also offer you official-looking immigration cards for a fee. These are fakes. Don't buy them.

Instructions

What Is This Form?

This form, the N-400, is an application for United States citizenship (naturalization). For more information about the naturalization process and eligibility requirements, please read *A Guide to Naturalization* (M-476). If you do not already have a copy of the *Guide*, you can get a copy from:

- the INS Web Site (www.ins.usdoj.gov);
- the National Customer Service Center (NCSC) telephone line at 1-800-375-5283 (TTY: 1-800-767-1833); or
- your local INS office.

Who Should Use This Form?

To use this form you must be at least 18 years old. You must also be **ONE** of the following:

(1) A Lawful Permanent Resident for at least 5 years;

(2) A Lawful Permanent Resident for at least 3 years
AND
- you have been married to and living with the same U.S. citizen for the last 3 years,
AND
- your spouse has been a U.S. citizen for the last 3 years;

(3) A person who has served in the U.S. Armed Forces
AND
- you are a Lawful Permanent Resident with at least 3 years of U.S. Armed Forces service **and** you are either on active duty or filing within 6 months of honorable discharge
OR
- you served during a period of recognized hostilities and enlisted or re-enlisted in the United States (you do not need to be a Lawful Permanent Resident);

(4) A member of one of several other groups who are eligible to apply for naturalization (for example, persons who are nationals but not citizens of the United States). For more information about these groups, please see the *Guide*.

Who Should NOT Use This Form?

In certain cases, a person who was born outside of the United States to U.S. citizen parents is already a citizen and does not need to apply for naturalization. To find out more information about this type of citizenship and whether you should file a Form N-600, "Application for Certificate of Citizenship," read the *Guide*.

Other permanent residents under 18 years of age may be eligible for U.S. citizenship if their U.S. citizen parent or parents file a Form N-600 application in their behalf. For more information, see "Frequently Asked Questions" in the *Guide*.

When Am I Eligible To Apply?

You may apply for naturalization when you meet **all** the requirements to become a U.S. citizen. The section of the *Guide* called "Who is Eligible for Naturalization" and the Eligibility Worksheet found in the back of the *Guide* are tools to help you determine whether you are eligible to apply for naturalization. You should complete the Worksheet before filling out this N-400 application.

If you are applying based on 5 years as a Lawful Permanent Resident or based on 3 years as a Lawful Permanent Resident married to a U.S. citizen, you may apply for naturalization up to 90 days before you meet the "continuous residence" requirement. You must meet all other requirements at the time that you file your application with us.

Certain applicants have different English and civics testing requirements based on their age and length of lawful permanent residence **at the time of filing**. If you are over 50 years of age and have lived in the United States as a lawful permanent resident for periods totaling at least 20 years or if you are over 55 years of age and have lived in the United States as a lawful permanent resident for periods totaling at least 15 years, you do not have to take the English test but you do have to take the civics test in the language of your choice.

Form N-400 Instructions (Rev. 07/23/02)N

Figure 4

If you are over 65 years of age and have lived in the United States as a lawful permanent resident for periods totaling at least 20 years, you do not have to take the English test but you do have to take a simpler version of the civics test in the language of your choice.

What Does It Cost To Apply For Naturalization and How Do I Pay?

For information on fees and form of payment, see the *Guide* insert titled "Current Naturalization Fees." Your fee is not refundable, even if you withdraw your application or it is denied.

If you are unable to pay the naturalization application fee, you may apply in writing for a fee waiver. For information about the fee waiver process, call the NCSC telephone line at 1-800-375-5283 (TTY: 1-800-767- 1833) or see the INS Web Site (www.ins.usdoj.gov) section called "Forms and Fees."

What Do I Send With My Application?

All applicants must send certain documents with their application. For information on the documents and other information you must send with your application, see the Document Checklist in the *Guide*.

Where Do I Send My Application?

You must send your N-400 application and supporting documents to an Immigration and Naturalization Service (INS) Service Center. To find the Service Center address you should use, read the section in the *Guide* called "Completing Your Application and Getting Photographed."

Applicants outside the United States who are applying on the basis of their military service should follow the instructions of their designated point of contact at a U.S. military installation.

How Do I Complete This Application?

- Please print clearly or type your answers using CAPITAL letters in each box.

- Use black or blue ink.

- **Write your INS "A"- number on the top right hand corner of each page.** Use your INS "A"- number on your Permanent Resident Card (formerly known as the Alien Registration or "Green" Card). To locate your "A"- number, see the sample Permanent Resident Cards in the *Guide*. The "A" number on your card consists of 7 to 9 numbers, depending on when your record was created. If the "A"- number on your card has fewer than 9 numbers, place enough zeros before the first number to make a *total of 9 numbers* on the application. For example, write card number A1234567 as A001234567, but write card number A12345678 as A012345678.

- If a question does not apply to you, write **N/A** (meaning "Not Applicable") in the space provided.

- If you need extra space to answer any item:
  - Attach a separate sheet of paper (or more sheets if needed);
  - Write your name, your "A"- number, and "N-400" on the top right corner of the sheet; and
  - Write the number of each question for which you are providing additional information.

Step-by-Step Instructions

This form is divided into 14 parts. The information below will help you fill out the form.

Part 1. Your Name *(the Person Applying for Naturalization)*

A. **Your current legal name -** Your current legal name is the name on your birth certificate unless it has been changed after birth by a legal action such as a marriage or court order.

Form N-400 Instructions (Rev. 07/23/02)N Page 2

Figure 4 (cont.)

B. **Your name exactly as it appears on your Permanent Resident Card** *(if different from above)* -- Write your name exactly as it appears on your card, even if it is misspelled.

C. **Other names you have used** - If you have used any other names in your life, write them in this section. If you need more space, use a separate sheet of paper.

If you have NEVER used a different name, write "N/A" in the space for "Family Name *(Last Name)*."

D. **Name change** *(optional)* - A court can allow a change in your name when you are being naturalized. A name change does not become final until a court naturalizes you. For more information regarding a name change, see the *Guide*.

If you want a court to change your name at a naturalization oath ceremony, check "Yes" and complete this section. If you do not want to change your name, check "No" and go to Part 2.

Part 2. Information About Your Eligibility

Check the box that shows why you are eligible to apply for naturalization. If the basis for your eligibility is not described in one of the first three boxes, check "Other" and briefly write the basis for your application on the lines provided.

Part 3. Information About You

A. **Social Security Number** - Print your Social Security number. If you do not have one, write "N/A" in the space provided.

B. **Date of Birth** - Always use eight numbers to show your date of birth. Write the date in this order: Month, Day, Year. For example, write May 1, 1958 as 05/01/1958.

C. **Date You Became a Permanent Resident** - Write the official date when your lawful permanent residence began, as shown on your Permanent Resident Card. To help locate the date on your card, see the sample Permanent Resident Cards in the *Guide*. Write the date in this order: Month, Day, Year. For example, write August 9, 1988 as 08/09/1988.

D. **Country of Birth** - Write the name of the country where you were born. Write the name of the country even if it no longer exists.

E. **Country of Nationality** - Write the name of the country where you are currently a citizen or national. Write the name of the country even if it no longer exists.

- If you are stateless, write the name of the country where you were last a citizen or national.

- If you are a citizen or national of more than one country, write the name of the foreign country that issued your last passport.

F. **Citizenship of Parents** - Check "Yes" if either of your parents is a U.S. citizen. If you answer "Yes," you may already be a citizen. For more information, see "Frequently Asked Questions" in the *Guide*.

G. **Current Marital Status** - Check the marital status you have on the date you are filing this application. If you are currently not married, but had a prior marriage that was annulled (declared by a court to be invalid) check "Other" and explain it.

H. **Request for Disability Waiver** - If you have a medical disability or impairment that you believe qualifies you for a waiver of the tests of English and/or U.S. government and history, check "Yes" and attach a properly completed Form N-648. If you ask for this waiver it does not guarantee that you will be excused from the testing requirements. For more information about this waiver, see the *Guide*.

I. **Request for Disability Accommodations** - We will make every reasonable effort to help applicants with disabilities complete the naturalization process. For example, if you use a wheelchair, we will make sure that you can be fingerprinted and interviewed, and can attend a naturalization ceremony at a location that is wheelchair accessible. If you are deaf or hearing impaired and need a sign language interpreter, we will make arrangements with you to have one at your interview.

Form N-400 Instructions (Rev. 07/23/02)N Page 3

Figure 4 (cont.)

If you believe you will need us to modify or change the naturalization process for you, check the box or write in the space the kind of accommodation you need. If you need more space, use a separate sheet of paper. You do not need to send us a Form N-648 to request an accommodation. You only need to send a Form N-648 to request a waiver of the test of English and/or civics.

We consider requests for accommodations on a case-by-case basis. Asking for an accommodation will not affect your eligibility for citizenship.

Part 4. Addresses and Telephone Numbers

A. **Home Address** - Give the address where you now live. Do NOT put post office (P.O.) box numbers here.

B. **Mailing Address** - If your mailing address is the same as your home address, write "same." If your mailing address is different from your home address, write it in this part.

C. **Telephone Numbers (optional)** - If you give us your telephone numbers and e-mail address, we can contact you about your application more quickly. If you are hearing impaired and use a TTY telephone connection, please indicate this by writing "(TTY)" after the telephone number.

Part 5. Information for Criminal Records Search

The Federal Bureau of Investigation (FBI) will use the information in this section, together with your fingerprints, to search for criminal records. Although the results of this search may affect your eligibility, we do NOT make naturalization decisions based on your gender, race, or physical description.

For each item, check the box or boxes that best describes you. The categories are those used by the FBI. Note, you can select one or more.

Part 6. Information About Your Residence and Employment

A. Write every address where you have lived during the last 5 years (including in other countries).

Begin with where you live now. Include the dates you lived in those places. For example, write May 1998 to June 1999 as 05/1998 to 06/1999.

If you need separate sheets of paper to complete section A or B or any other questions on this application, be sure to follow the Instructions in **"How Do I Complete This Application?"** above.

B. List where you have worked (or, if you were a student, the schools you have attended) during the last 5 years. Include military service. If you worked for yourself, write "self employed." Begin with your most recent job. Also, write the dates when you worked or studied in each place.

Part 7. Time Outside the United States *(Including Trips to Canada and Mexico and the Caribbean)*

A. Write the total number of days you spent outside of the United States (including on military service) during the last 5 years. Count the days of every trip that lasted 24 hours or longer.

B. Write the number of trips you have taken outside the United States during the last 5 years. Count every trip that lasted 24 hours or longer.

C. Provide the requested information for every trip that you have taken outside the United States since you became a Lawful Permanent Resident. Begin with your most recent trip.

Part 8. Information About Your Marital History

A. Write the number of times you have been married. Include any annulled marriages. If you were married to the same spouse more than one time, count each time as a separate marriage.

B. If you are now married, provide information about your current spouse.

C. Check the box to indicate whether your current spouse is a U.S. citizen.

Form N-400 Instructions (Rev. 07/23/02)N Page 4

Figure 4 (cont.)

D. If your spouse is a citizen through naturalization, give the date and place of naturalization. If your spouse regained U.S. citizenship, write the date and place the citizenship was regained.

E. If your spouse is not a U.S. citizen, complete this section.

F. If you were married before, give information about your former spouse or spouses. In question F.2, check the box showing the immigration status your former spouse had during your marriage. If the spouse was not a U.S. citizen or a Lawful Permanent Resident at that time check "Other" and explain. For question F.5, if your marriage was annulled, check "Other" and explain. If you were married to the same spouse more than one time, write about each marriage separately.

G. For any prior marriages of your current spouse, follow the instructions in section F above.

Note: If you or your present spouse had more than one prior marriage, provide the same information required by section F and section G about every additional marriage on a separate sheet of paper.

Part 9. Information About Your Children

A. Write the total number of sons and daughters you have had. Count **all** of your children, regardless of whether they are:
- alive, missing, or dead;
- born in other countries or in the United States;
- under 18 years old or adults;
- married or unmarried;
- living with you or elsewhere;
- stepsons or stepdaughters or legally adopted; or
- born when you were not married.

B. Write information about all your sons and daughters. In the last column ("Location"), write:

- "with me" - if the son or daughter is currently living with you;

- the street address and state or country where the son or daughter lives - if the son or daughter is NOT currently living with you; or

- "missing" or "dead" - if that son or daughter is missing or dead.

If you need space to list information about additional sons and daughters, attach a separate sheet of paper.

Part 10. Additional Questions

Answer each question by checking "Yes" or "No." If ANY part of a question applies to you, you must answer "Yes." For example, if you were never arrested but *were* once detained by a police officer, check "Yes" to the question "Have you ever been arrested or detained by a law enforcement officer?" and attach a written explanation.

We will use this information to determine your eligibility for citizenship. Answer every question honestly and accurately. If you do not, we may deny your application for lack of good moral character. Answering "Yes" to one of these questions does not always cause an application to be denied. For more information on eligibility, please see the *Guide*.

Part 11. Your Signature

After reading the statement in Part 11, you must sign and date it. You should sign your full name without abbreviating it or using initials. The signature must be legible. Your application may be returned to you if it is not signed.

If you cannot sign your name in English, sign in your native language. If you are unable to write in any language, sign your name with an "X."

NOTE: A designated representative may sign this section on behalf an applicant who qualifies for a waiver of the Oath of Allegiance because of a development or physical impairment (see *Guide* for more information). In such a case the designated representative should write the name of the applicant and then sign his or her own name followed by the words "Designated Representative." The information attested to by the Designated Representative is subject to the same penalties discussed on page 6 of these Instructions.

Figure 4 (cont.)

Part 12. Signature of Person Who Prepared This Application for You

If someone filled out this form for you, he or she must complete this section.

Part 13. Signature at Interview

Do NOT complete this part. You will be asked to complete this part at your interview.

Part 14. Oath of Allegiance

Do NOT complete this part. You will be asked to complete this part at your interview.

If we approve your application, you must take this Oath of Allegiance to become a citizen. In limited cases you can take a modified Oath. The Oath requirement cannot be waived unless you are unable to understand its meaning because of a physical or developmental disability or mental impairment. For more information, see the *Guide.* Your signature on this form only indicates that you have no objections to taking the Oath of Allegiance. **It does not mean that you have taken the Oath or that you are naturalized**. If the INS approves your application for naturalization, you must attend an oath ceremony and take the Oath of Allegiance to the United States.

Penalties

If you knowingly and willfully falsify or conceal a material fact or submit a false document with this request, we will deny your application for naturalization and may deny any other immigration benefit. In addition, you will face severe penalties provided by law and may be subject to a removal proceeding or criminal prosecution.

If we grant you citizenship after you falsify or conceal a material fact or submit a false document with this request, your naturalization may be revoked.

Privacy Act Notice

We ask for the information on this form and for other documents to determine your eligibility for naturalization. Form N-400 processes are generally covered in 8 U.S.C. 1421 through 1430 and 1436 through 1449. We may provide information from your application to other government agencies.

Paperwork Reduction Act Notice

A person is not required to respond to a collection of information unless it displays a valid OMB control number. We try to create forms and instructions that are accurate, can be easily understood and which impose the least possible burden on you to provide us with the information. Often this is difficult because some immigration laws are very complex. The estimated average time to complete and file this form is computed as follows: (1) 2 hours and 8 minutes to learn about and complete the form; (2) 4 hours to assemble and file the information - for a total estimated average of 6 hours and 8 minutes per application. If you have comments about the accuracy of this estimate or suggestions to make this form simpler, you can write to the Immigration and Naturalization Service, HQRFS, 425 I Street, N.W., Room 4034, Washington, DC 20536; OMB No. 1115-0009. **DO NOT MAIL YOUR COMPLETED APPLICATION TO THIS ADDRESS.**

Form N-400 Instructions (Rev. 07/23/02)N Page 6

Figure 4 (cont.)

Fill out this form in **pencil**.

Print clearly or type your answers using CAPITAL letters. Failure to print clearly may delay your application. Use black or blue ink.

Part 1. Your Name *(The Person Applying for Naturalization)*

Write your INS "A"- number here:

A . . . .

A. Your current legal name.

Family Name *(Last Name)*

Given Name *(First Name)*   Full Middle Name *(If applicable)*

FOR INS USE ONLY

Bar Code	Date Stamp

Remarks

B. Your name **exactly** as it appears on your Permanent Resident Card.

Family Name *(Last Name)*

Given Name *(First Name)*   Full Middle Name *(If applicable)*

C. If you have ever used other names, provide them below.

Family Name *(Last Name)*	Given Name *(First Name)*	Middle Name

D. Name change *(optional)*

Please read the Instructions before you decide whether to change your name.

1. Would you like to legally change your name?   ☐ Yes   ☐ No

2. If "Yes," print the new name you would like to use. Do not use initials or abbreviations when writing your new name.

Family Name *(Last Name)*

Given Name *(First Name)*   Full Middle Name

Action

Part 2. Information About Your Eligibility   *(Check Only One)*

I am at least 18 years old **AND**

A. ☐ I have been a Lawful Permanent Resident of the United States for at least 5 years.

B. ☐ I have been a Lawful Permanent Resident of the United States for at least 3 years, AND I have been married to and living with the same U.S. citizen for the last 3 years, AND my spouse has been a U.S. citizen for the last 3 years.

C. ☐ I am applying on the basis of qualifying military service.

D. ☐ Other *(Please explain)* _____

Form N-400 (Rev. 07/23/02)N

Figure 5

Part 3. Information About You

Write your INS "A"- number here:

A _ _ _ _ _ _ _ _ _ _ _

A. Social Security Number

_ _ _ - _ _ - _ _ _ _

B. Date of Birth *(Month/Day/Year)*

_ _ / _ _ / _ _ _ _

C. Date You Became a Permanent Resident *(Month/Day/Year)*

_ _ / _ _ / _ _ _ _

D. Country of Birth

E. Country of Nationality

F. Are either of your parents U.S. citizens? *(if yes, see Instructions)* ☐ Yes ☐ No

G. What is your current marital status? ☐ Single, Never Married ☐ Married ☐ Divorced ☐ Widowed

☐ Marriage Annulled or Other *(Explain)* _____

H. Are you requesting a waiver of the English and/or U.S. History and Government requirements based on a disability or impairment and attaching a Form N-648 with your application? ☐ Yes ☐ No

I. Are you requesting an accommodation to the naturalization process because of a disability or impairment? *(See Instructions for some examples of accommodations.)* ☐ Yes ☐ No

If you answered "Yes", check the box below that applies:

☐ I am deaf or hearing impaired and need a sign language interpreter who uses the following language: _____

☐ I use a wheelchair.

☐ I am blind or sight impaired.

☐ I will need another type of accommodation. Please explain: _____

_____

_____

Part 4. Addresses and Telephone Numbers

A. Home Address - Street Number and Name *(Do NOT write a P.O. Box in this space)*

Apartment Number

City | County | State | ZIP Code | Country

B. Care of

Mailing Address - Street Number and Name *(If different from home address)*

Apartment Number

City | State | ZIP Code | Country

C. Daytime Phone Number *(If any)*

( )

Evening Phone Number *(If any)*

( )

E-mail Address *(If any)*

Figure 5 (cont.)

Part 5. Information for Criminal Records Search

Write your INS "A"- number here:

A _ _ _ _ _ _ _ _ _

Note: The categories below are those required by the FBI. See Instructions for more information.

A. Gender

☐ Male ☐ Female

B. Height

Feet	Inches

C. Weight

Pounds

D. Are you Hispanic or Latino? ☐ Yes ☐ No

E. Race *(Select one or more.)*

☐ White ☐ Asian ☐ Black or African American ☐ American Indian or Alaskan Native ☐ Native Hawaiian or Other Pacific Islander

F. Hair color

☐ Black ☐ Brown ☐ Blonde ☐ Gray ☐ White ☐ Red ☐ Sandy ☐ Bald (No Hair)

G. Eye color

☐ Brown ☐ Blue ☐ Green ☐ Hazel ☐ Gray ☐ Black ☐ Pink ☐ Maroon ☐ Other

Part 6. Information About Your Residence and Employment

A. Where have you lived during the last 5 years? Begin with where you live now and then list every place you lived for the last 5 years. If you need more space, use a separate sheet of paper.

Street Number and Name, Apartment Number, City, State, Zip Code and Country	Dates *(Month/Year)*	
	From	To
Current Home Address - Same as Part 4.A	_ _ / _ _ _ _	Present
	_ _ / _ _ _ _	_ _ / _ _ _ _
	_ _ / _ _ _ _	_ _ / _ _ _ _
	_ _ / _ _ _ _	_ _ / _ _ _ _
	_ _ / _ _ _ _	_ _ / _ _ _ _

B. Where have you worked (or, if you were a student, what schools did you attend) during the last 5 years? Include military service. Begin with your current or latest employer and then list every place you have worked or studied for the last 5 years. If you need more space, use a separate sheet of paper.

Employer or School Name	Employer or School Address *(Street, City and State)*	Dates *(Month/Year)*		Your Occupation
		From	To	
		_ _ / _ _ _ _	_ _ / _ _ _ _	
		_ _ / _ _ _ _	_ _ / _ _ _ _	
		_ _ / _ _ _ _	_ _ / _ _ _ _	
		_ _ / _ _ _ _	_ _ / _ _ _ _	
		_ _ / _ _ _ _	_ _ / _ _ _ _	

Form N-400 (Rev. 07/23/02)N Page 3

Figure 5 (cont.)

A. How many total days did you spend outside of the United States during the past 5 years? [_____] days

B. How many trips of 24 hours or more have you taken outside of the United States during the past 5 years? [_____] trips

C. List below all the trips of 24 hours or more that you have taken outside of the United States since becoming a Lawful Permanent Resident. Begin with your most recent trip. If you need more space, use a separate sheet of paper.

Date You Left the United States (Month/Day/Year)	Date You Returned to the United States (Month/Day/Year)	Did Trip Last 6 Months or More?	Countries to Which You Traveled	Total Days Out of the United States
_ _ / _ _ / _ _ _ _	_ _ / _ _ / _ _ _ _	☐ Yes ☐ No		
_ _ / _ _ / _ _ _ _	_ _ / _ _ / _ _ _ _	☐ Yes ☐ No		
_ _ / _ _ / _ _ _ _	_ _ / _ _ / _ _ _ _	☐ Yes ☐ No		
_ _ / _ _ / _ _ _ _	_ _ / _ _ / _ _ _ _	☐ Yes ☐ No		
_ _ / _ _ / _ _ _ _	_ _ / _ _ / _ _ _ _	☐ Yes ☐ No		
_ _ / _ _ / _ _ _ _	_ _ / _ _ / _ _ _ _	☐ Yes ☐ No		
_ _ / _ _ / _ _ _ _	_ _ / _ _ / _ _ _ _	☐ Yes ☐ No		
_ _ / _ _ / _ _ _ _	_ _ / _ _ / _ _ _ _	☐ Yes ☐ No		
_ _ / _ _ / _ _ _ _	_ _ / _ _ / _ _ _ _	☐ Yes ☐ No		
_ _ / _ _ / _ _ _ _	_ _ / _ _ / _ _ _ _	☐ Yes ☐ No		

Part 8. Information About Your Marital History

A. How many times have you been married (including annulled marriages)? [_____] If you have NEVER been married, go to Part 9.

B. If you are now married, give the following information about your spouse:

1. Spouse's Family Name *(Last Name)*   Given Name *(First Name)*   Full Middle Name *(If applicable)*

2. Date of Birth *(Month/Day/Year)*   3. Date of Marriage *(Month/Day/Year)*   4. Spouse's Social Security Number

_ _ / _ _ / _ _ _ _   _ _ / _ _ / _ _ _ _   _ _ _ - _ _ - _ _ _ _

5. Home Address - Street Number and Name   Apartment Number

City   State   ZIP Code

Figure 5 (cont.)

Write your INS "A"- number here:

A _ _ _ _ _ _ _ _ _ _ _

C. Is your spouse a U.S. citizen? ☐ Yes ☐ No

D. If your spouse is a U.S. citizen, give the following information:

1. When did your spouse become a U.S. citizen? ☐ At Birth ☐ Other

If "Other," give the following information:

2. Date your spouse became a U.S. citizen

_ _/_ _/_ _ _ _

3. Place your spouse became a U.S. citizen *(Please see Instructions)*

City and State

E. If your spouse is NOT a U.S. citizen, give the following information :

1. Spouse's Country of Citizenship

2. Spouse's INS "A"- Number *(If applicable)*

A _ _ _ _ _ _ _ _ _

3. Spouse's Immigration Status

☐ Lawful Permanent Resident ☐ Other _____

F. If you were married before, provide the following information about your prior spouse. If you have more than one previous marriage, use a separate sheet of paper to provide the information requested in questions 1-5 below.

1. Prior Spouse's Family Name *(Last Name)* | Given Name *(First Name)* | Full Middle Name *(If applicable)*

2. Prior Spouse's Immigration Status

☐ U.S. Citizen
☐ Lawful Permanent Resident
☐ Other _____

3. Date of Marriage *(Month/Day/Year)*

_ _/_ _/_ _ _ _

4. Date Marriage Ended *(Month/Day/Year)*

_ _/_ _/_ _ _ _

5. How Marriage Ended

☐ Divorce ☐ Spouse Died ☐ Other _____

G. How many times has your current spouse been married (including annulled marriages)? _____

If your spouse has EVER been married before, give the following information about **your spouse's** prior marriage.
If your spouse has more than one previous marriage, use a separate sheet of paper to provide the information requested in questions 1 - 5 below.

1. Prior Spouse's Family Name *(Last Name)* | Given Name *(First Name)* | Full Middle Name *(If applicable)*

2. Prior Spouse's Immigration Status

☐ U.S. Citizen
☐ Lawful Permanent Resident
☐ Other _____

3. Date of Marriage *(Month/Day/Year)*

_ _/_ _/_ _ _ _

4. Date Marriage Ended *(Month/Day/Year)*

_ _/_ _/_ _ _ _

5. How Marriage Ended

☐ Divorce ☐ Spouse Died ☐ Other _____

Form N-400 (Rev. 07/23/02)N Page 5

Figure 5 (cont.)

| Part 9. Information About Your Children | Write your INS "A"- number here: A _ _ _ _ _ _ _ _ _ |

A. How many sons and daughters have you had? For more information on which sons and daughters you should include and how to complete this section, see the Instructions.

B. Provide the following information about all of your sons and daughters. If you need more space, use a separate sheet of paper.

Full Name of Son or Daughter	Date of Birth *(Month/Day/Year)*	INS "A"- number *(if child has one)*	Country of Birth	Current Address *(Street, City, State & Country)*
	_ _ / _ / _ _ _ _	A_ _ _ _ _ _ _ _		
	_ _ / _ / _ _ _ _	A_ _ _ _ _ _ _ _		
	_ _ / _ / _ _ _ _	A_ _ _ _ _ _ _ _		
	_ _ / _ / _ _ _ _	A_ _ _ _ _ _ _ _		
	_ _ / _ / _ _ _ _	A_ _ _ _ _ _ _ _		
	_ _ / _ / _ _ _ _	A_ _ _ _ _ _ _ _		
	_ _ / _ / _ _ _ _	A_ _ _ _ _ _ _ _		
	_ _ / _ / _ _ _ _	A_ _ _ _ _ _ _ _		

| Part 10. Additional Questions |

Please answer questions 1 through 14. If you answer "Yes" to any of these questions, include a written explanation with this form. Your written explanation should (1) explain why your answer was "Yes," and (2) provide any additional information that helps to explain your answer.

A. General Questions

1. Have you **EVER** claimed to be a U.S. citizen *(in writing or any other way)*?   ☐ Yes   ☐ No

2. Have you **EVER** registered to vote in any Federal, state, or local election in the United States?   ☐ Yes   ☐ No

3. Have you **EVER** voted in any Federal, state, or local election in the United States?   ☐ Yes   ☐ No

4. Since becoming a Lawful Permanent Resident, have you **EVER** failed to file a required Federal, state, or local tax return?   ☐ Yes   ☐ No

5. Do you owe any Federal, state, or local taxes that are overdue?   ☐ Yes   ☐ No

6. Do you have any title of nobility in any foreign country?   ☐ Yes   ☐ No

7. Have you ever been declared legally incompetent or been confined to a mental institution within the last 5 years?   ☐ Yes   ☐ No

Form N-400 (Rev. 07/23/02)N Page 6

Figure 5 (cont.)

Write your INS "A"- number here:

A __ __ __ __ __ __ __ __ __ __

B. Affiliations

8. a. Have you **EVER** been a member of or associated with any organization, association, fund, foundation, party, club, society, or similar group in the United States or in any other place?   ☐ Yes ☐ No

    b. If you answered "Yes," list the name of each group below. If you need more space, attach the names of the other group(s) on a separate sheet of paper.

Name of Group	Name of Group
1.	6.
2.	7.
3.	8.
4.	9.
5.	10.

9. Have you **EVER** been a member of or in any way associated *(either directly or indirectly)* with:

    a. The Communist Party?   ☐ Yes ☐ No

    b. Any other totalitarian party?   ☐ Yes ☐ No

    c. A terrorist organization?   ☐ Yes ☐ No

10. Have you **EVER** advocated *(either directly or indirectly)* the overthrow of any government by force or violence?   ☐ Yes ☐ No

11. Have you **EVER** persecuted *(either directly or indirectly)* any person because of race, religion, national origin, membership in a particular social group, or political opinion?   ☐ Yes ☐ No

12. Between March 23, 1933, and May 8, 1945, did you work for or associate in any way *(either directly or indirectly)* with:

    a. The Nazi government of Germany?   ☐ Yes ☐ No

    b. Any government in any area (1) occupied by, (2) allied with, or (3) established with the help of the Nazi government of Germany?   ☐ Yes ☐ No

    c. Any German, Nazi, or S.S. military unit, paramilitary unit, self-defense unit, vigilante unit, citizen unit, police unit, government agency or office, extermination camp, concentration camp, prisoner of war camp, prison, labor camp, or transit camp?   ☐ Yes ☐ No

C. Continuous Residence

Since becoming a Lawful Permanent Resident of the United States:

13. Have you **EVER** called yourself a "nonresident" on a Federal, state, or local tax return?   ☐ Yes ☐ No

14. Have you **EVER** failed to file a Federal, state, or local tax return because you considered yourself to be a "nonresident"?   ☐ Yes ☐ No

Form N-400 (Rev. 07/23/02)N Page 7

Figure 5 (cont.)

D. Good Moral Character

For the purposes of this application, you must answer "Yes" to the following questions, if applicable, even if your records were sealed or otherwise cleared or if anyone, including a judge, law enforcement officer, or attorney, told you that you no longer have a record.

15. Have you **EVER** committed a crime or offense for which you were NOT arrested? ☐ Yes ☐ No

16. Have you **EVER** been arrested, cited, or detained by any law enforcement officer (including INS and military officers) for any reason? ☐ Yes ☐ No

17. Have you **EVER** been charged with committing any crime or offense? ☐ Yes ☐ No

18. Have you **EVER** been convicted of a crime or offense? ☐ Yes ☐ No

19. Have you **EVER** been placed in an alternative sentencing or a rehabilitative program (for example: diversion, deferred prosecution, withheld adjudication, deferred adjudication)? ☐ Yes ☐ No

20. Have you **EVER** received a suspended sentence, been placed on probation, or been paroled? ☐ Yes ☐ No

21. Have you **EVER** been in jail or prison? ☐ Yes ☐ No

If you answered "Yes" to any of questions 15 through 21, complete the following table. If you need more space, use a separate sheet of paper to give the same information.

Why were you arrested, cited, detained, or charged?	Date arrested, cited, detained, or charged? *(Month/Day/Year)*	Where were you arrested, cited, detained or charged? *(City, State, Country)*	Outcome or disposition of the arrest, citation, detention or charge *(No charges filed, charges dismissed, jail, probation, etc.)*

Answer questions 22 through 33. If you answer "Yes" to any of these questions, attach (1) your written explanation why your answer was "Yes," and (2) any additional information or documentation that helps explain your answer.

22. Have you **EVER**:

   a. been a habitual drunkard? ☐ Yes ☐ No

   b. been a prostitute, or procured anyone for prostitution? ☐ Yes ☐ No

   c. sold or smuggled controlled substances, illegal drugs or narcotics? ☐ Yes ☐ No

   d. been married to more than one person at the same time? ☐ Yes ☐ No

   e. helped anyone enter or try to enter the United States illegally? ☐ Yes ☐ No

   f. gambled illegally or received income from illegal gambling? ☐ Yes ☐ No

   g. failed to support your dependents or to pay alimony? ☐ Yes ☐ No

23. Have you **EVER** given false or misleading information to any U.S. government official while applying for any immigration benefit or to prevent deportation, exclusion, or removal? ☐ Yes ☐ No

24. Have you **EVER** lied to any U.S. government official to gain entry or admission into the United States? ☐ Yes ☐ No

Form N-400 (Rev. 07/23/02)N Page 8

Figure 5 (cont.)

Write your INS "A"- number here:

A _ _ _ _ _ _ _ _ _

E. Removal, Exclusion, and Deportation Proceedings

25. Are removal, exclusion, rescission or deportation proceedings pending against you?　□ Yes　□ No

26. Have you **EVER** been removed, excluded, or deported from the United States?　□ Yes　□ No

27. Have you **EVER** been ordered to be removed, excluded, or deported from the United States?　□ Yes　□ No

28. Have you **EVER** applied for any kind of relief from removal, exclusion, or deportation?　□ Yes　□ No

F. Military Service

29. Have you **EVER** served in the U.S. Armed Forces?　□ Yes　□ No

30. Have you **EVER** left the United States to avoid being drafted into the U.S. Armed Forces?　□ Yes　□ No

31. Have you **EVER** applied for any kind of exemption from military service in the U.S. Armed Forces?　□ Yes　□ No

32. Have you **EVER** deserted from the U.S. Armed Forces?　□ Yes　□ No

G. Selective Service Registration

33. Are you a male who lived in the United States at any time between your 18th and 26th birthdays
in any status except as a lawful nonimmigrant?　□ Yes　□ No

If you answered "NO", go on to question 34.

If you answered "YES", provide the information below.

If you answered "YES", but you did NOT register with the Selective Service System and are still under 26 years of age, you must register before you apply for naturalization, so that you can complete the information below:

Date Registered (Month/Day/Year) [   ]　　Selective Service Number _ _ / _ _ _ _ _ _ /

If you answered "YES", but you did NOT register with the Selective Service and you are now 26 years old or older, attach a statement explaining why you did not register.

H. Oath Requirements *(See Part 14 for the text of the oath)*

Answer questions 34 through 39. If you answer "No" to any of these questions, attach (1) your written explanation why the answer was "No" and (2) any additional information or documentation that helps to explain your answer.

34. Do you support the Constitution and form of government of the United States?　□ Yes　□ No

35. Do you understand the full Oath of Allegiance to the United States?　□ Yes　□ No

36. Are you willing to take the full Oath of Allegiance to the United States?　□ Yes　□ No

37. If the law requires it, are you willing to bear arms on behalf of the United States?　□ Yes　□ No

38. If the law requires it, are you willing to perform noncombatant services in the U.S. Armed Forces?　□ Yes　□ No

39. If the law requires it, are you willing to perform work of national importance under civilian direction?　□ Yes　□ No

Form N-400 (Rev. 07/23/02)N Page 9

Figure 5 (cont.)

Part 11. Your Signature

Write your INS "A"- number here:

A _ _ _ _ _ _ _ _ _ _

I certify, under penalty of perjury under the laws of the United States of America, that this application, and the evidence submitted with it, are all true and correct. I authorize the release of any information which INS needs to determine my eligibility for naturalization.

Your Signature

Date *(Month/Day/Year)*

_ _ / _ _ / _ _ _ _

Part 12. Signature of Person Who Prepared This Application for You *(if applicable)*

I declare under penalty of perjury that I prepared this application at the request of the above person. The answers provided are based on information of which I have personal knowledge and/or were provided to me by the above named person in response to the *exact questions* contained on this form.

Preparer's Printed Name

Preparer's Signature

Date *(Month/Day/Year)*

_ _ / _ _ / _ _ _ _

Preparer's Firm or Organization Name *(If applicable)*

Preparer's Daytime Phone Number

( )

Preparer's Address - Street Number and Name

City

State

ZIP Code

Do Not Complete Parts 13 and 14 Until an INS Officer Instructs You To Do So

Part 13. Signature at Interview

I swear (affirm) and certify under penalty of perjury under the laws of the United States of America that I know that the contents of this application for naturalization subscribed by me, including corrections numbered 1 through _____ and the evidence submitted by me numbered pages 1 through _____ , are true and correct to the best of my knowledge and belief.

Subscribed to and sworn to (affirmed) before me

Officer's Printed Name or Stamp

Date *(Month/Day/Year)*

Complete Signature of Applicant

Officer's Signature

Part 14. Oath of Allegiance

If your application is approved, you will be scheduled for a public oath ceremony at which time you will be required to take the following oath of allegiance immediately prior to becoming a naturalized citizen. By signing , you acknowledge your willingness and ability to take this oath:

I hereby declare, on oath, that I absolutely and entirely renounce and abjure all allegiance and fidelity to any foreign prince, potentate, state, or sovereignty, of whom or which which I have heretofore been a subject or citizen;

that I will support and defend the Constitution and laws of the United States of America against all enemies, foreign and domestic;

that I will bear true faith and allegiance to the same;

that I will bear arms on behalf of the United States when required by the law;

that I will perform noncombatant service in the Armed Forces of the United States when required by the law;

that I will perform work of national importance under civilian direction when required by the law; and

that I take this obligation freely, without any mental reservation or purpose of evasion; so help me God.

Printed Name of Applicant

Complete Signature of Applicant

Form N-400 (Rev. 07/23/02)N Page 10

Figure 5 (cont.)

Some Questions You May Have

How do I legalize my status?

If you have been living here for some time and feel you may not be eligible to become a citizen, do not give up hope. Under the Immigration Reform and Control Act of 1986, you may have already filed for temporary residence under the amnesty provisions. But even if you missed the date for filing, there are ways of adjusting, or legalizing, your status. In either case, if you are eligible to change from a temporary to a permanent resident, you may obtain Form I-485 or other appropriate forms by calling the USCIS at 1-800-870-3676 (free call). The fee for filing is $315. (See "Forms and Fees" section.)

What about my children?

Your natural or adopted children here with you may become citizens when you do, without filing any forms, if they are minors (under 18 years of age), unmarried, and legally admitted for permanent residence.

You may obtain a U.S. passport for your children as evidence of citizenship. If the children need further evidence of citizenship, you may submit an "Application for Certificate of Citizenship (Form N-600)."

I am not sure that I have *continuous* residence because I went back and forth to Italy during my mother's illness. Do I qualify?

If you have questions about your eligibility, you may want to seek advice from an immigration attorney or an immigrant assistance organization. Your local USCIS office can help you find one of these organizations.

Can I bring any of my family here?

As a permanent resident, you can petition for your spouse and unmarried children under age 21. When you become a citizen, you can do even more.

What can I do if I lose any of my naturalization papers or change my name?

A person whose Certificate of Citizenship has been lost, mutilated, or destroyed or a naturalized person whose name has been changed by a court or by marriage *after* naturalization may apply for a new paper. The application form (N-565) is available from the USCIS Forms Line at 1-800-870-3676 or on the Internet at *http://uscis.gov*. It should be filled out, following the instructions on the form, and taken or mailed to the local USCIS office, along with the required photographs and a check or money order for $210. Any documents that show the reason for the change of status should be submitted.

NOTE: If a person changes his or her name or marital status, there is no legal requirement to apply for a new certificate. This is the person's option.

If a person loses a Permanent Resident Card (green card), he or she must file Form I-90. This form is also available from the USCIS Forms Line at 1-800-870-3676. Again it should be carefully filled out, following the instructions on the form, and submitted with a check or money order for $185 to that office.

What do I do if I move after I send in my N-400?

You must notify USCIS of your change of address.

- You can change your address by phone. You can call 1-800-375-5283 from 8 a.m. to 6 p.m., Monday to Friday. <u>Or</u>,

- You can change your address by mail. You can call 1-800-870-3676 to request Form AR-11 (Alien's Change of Address Card) and mail it to the office where you sent your Form N-400.

It is very important to notify USCIS of the new address. If you do not do so, USCIS will not send your notifications to the right place. For instance, you may not receive information on where and when to get fingerprinted and you may not be aware of the date and place of your interview.

Step 2— Filing Your Form

You have completed the sample form. How does it look? Is it clear? If you needed to send it to the USCIS, would you be proud to do so? If so, then you are ready to go on to the real thing!

How you fill out each form is very important. You want very much to become an American citizen; therefore, you must do your best in applying for citizenship.

Forms must be typed or printed by hand in capital letters in black or blue ink. Care must be taken that even the last copy can be read. All necessary documents should be included. Send copies of the documents unless the USCIS asks for the originals.

Form N-400: Now Fill Out the Real Thing

First, take out your Permanent Resident Card. Your name, exactly as it is on the card, must be printed in Part 1. Be careful as you fill in your alien registration number and your social security number. If you are using a *different name* now, of if you used any other name in the past, that also goes in Part 1.

When you have completed your final form, you should mail it, with payment, to the appropriate regional office listed below. You may send it 3 months before you have the full residence time needed for your application.

Include a check or money order for $390 made out to the United States Citizenship and Immigration Services. ($320 is the application fee, and $70 is the fingerprinting fee.) Also send in a copy of both sides of your Permanent Resident Card and two recent color photographs. Make copies of your N-400. Keep your copies in a safe place. Now mail "the real thing" and wait. You will hear from the USCIS telling you where and when to go to be fingerprinted.

Here is the list of regional offices:

If you live in Alabama, Arkansas, Florida, Georgia, Kentucky, Louisiana, Mississippi, New Mexico, North Carolina, Oklahoma, South Carolina, Tennessee, or Texas, send your application to:

Texas Service Center
P.O. Box 851204
Mesquite, TX 75185-1204

If you live in Arizona, California, Hawaii, Nevada, Territory of Guam, or the Commonwealth of the Northern Mariana Islands, send your application to:

California Service Center
P.O. Box 10400
Laguna Niguel, CA 92607-0400

If you live in Alaska, Colorado, Idaho, Illinois, Indiana, Iowa, Kansas, Michigan, Minnesota, Missouri, Montana, Nebraska, North Dakota, Ohio, Oregon, South Dakota, Utah, Washington, Wisconsin, or Wyoming, send your application to:

Nebraska Service Center
P.O. Box 87400
Lincoln, NE 68501-7400

If you live in Connecticut, Delaware, District of Columbia, Maine, Maryland, Massachusetts, New Hampshire, New Jersey, New York, Pennsylvania, Rhode Island, Vermont, Virginia, West Virginia, Commonwealth of Puerto Rico, or the U.S. Virgin Islands, send your application to:

Vermont Service Center
75 Lower Weldon Street
St. Alban, VT 05479-0001

Note: If you are overseas and filing an N-400, you should send your application to the Service Center that serves the USCIS office where you want to be interviewed. For example, if you want to be interviewed in the Honolulu office, you should send your application to the California Service Center.

Important! Look for your state. Where will you mail your N-400?

Let's see what one of my students did. She was very excited! Telling the class "It is time!" three months before she reached the five-years residence required, she was ready to mail in her final Form N-400. She made copies of it after she checked everything carefully, and she addressed it to the regional center that would take care of it. During the time that she had been a legal permanent resident of the United States, she had not moved from her home in Brooklyn, New York. Therefore, she will receive information on where to go to get fingerprinted, and she will be aware of the date and place of her interview.

**Before you go on to the next step, read the questions
(and their answers) on the next three pages.
They will help you get ready for the interview.**

Probability Questions

Let's see where you are, as far as knowledge of your new country, its history, and the foundation of government here. See how many are easy for you! I call these *probability questions* because it is probable that you will be asked some of them at your naturalization interview. While that may be a long way off, it is best to have some idea and some practice in using the words of the naturalization examiner. *Do not try to memorize them!* These are typical questions asked by the naturalization examiner and sample answers that are acceptable.

1. **What is the form of government of the United States of America?**

   It is a democracy and a republic, which means that it is a government of the people, by the people, and for the people.

2. **How many states are there in the United States of America?**

   Fifty.

3. **What is the highest law of the United States of America?**

   The Constitution.

4. **What is the highest court of the United States of America?**

   The Supreme Court.

5. **Who is the president of the United States of America?**

   George W. Bush (as of January 2001).

6. **Who was the first president of the United States of America?**

   George Washington.

7. **Who was the president who freed the slaves?**

   Abraham Lincoln issued the Emancipation Proclamation.

8. **Why do we celebrate the Fourth of July?**

   The Fourth of July is Independence Day, the day the colonies declared their independence from England in 1776.

9. **What are the colors of the American flag?**

   Red, white, and blue.

10. **Describe the flag.**

    It has 13 stripes, one for each of the 13 original colonies; and it has 50 stars, one for each of the current states. The stars are white on a blue background.

11. **Who makes the laws for the United States?**

    Congress, made up of the Senate and the House of Representatives. The Senate has 100 members; the House of Representatives has 435.

12. **What is the Supreme Court?**

It is the highest court of the country. It interprets laws and declares unconstitutional any laws that are not in accordance with the Constitution. Such laws cannot remain in effect.

13. **Can the Constitution be changed?**

Yes, it can be changed by amendment.

14. **What is the Bill of Rights?**

The first 10 amendments to the Constitution that protect the rights of all Americans.

15. **What is the Fourteenth Amendment?**

This amendment, which took effect in 1868, provides important protection to all citizens. The first part of this amendment says: "All persons born or naturalized in the United States, and subject to the jurisdiction thereof, are citizens of the United States, and of the state wherein they reside. No State shall make or enforce any law which shall abridge the privileges or immunities of citizens of the United States; nor shall any State deprive any person of life, liberty, or property, without due process of law."

16. **What is the difference between the Bill of Rights and the Fourteenth Amendment?**

The Bill of Rights protects us from actions of the federal government, and the Fourteenth Amendment protects us from actions of the state as well.

17. **Who is the chief executive of the United States?**

The president.

18. **Who is the chief executive of the state?**

The governor.

19. **Are there governments other than the federal government?**

Yes. There are state and local governments.

20. **What is meant by "checks and balances" in the government of the United States?**

Each of the three departments of government has power to veto (or declare unconstitutional) the action of another. The Senate must approve some appointments made by the president. That is just one example.

21. **How is the president elected?**

By the people through the Electoral College, made up of representatives from each state. The candidate must receive a majority of votes in order to be elected.

22. **What is the term of office of a president?**

Four years.

23. What is the term of office of a senator? A congressman or -woman?

Six years for a senator. Two years for a congressman or -woman.

24. What is the cabinet?

The heads of the executive departments appointed by the president to advise him.

25. Who was Dr. Martin Luther King, Jr.?

A civil rights leader who was assassinated.

Step 3—Serious Study—English

Some time may have passed since you requested the forms. It seems a long wait. Be patient. Use this time to become more familiar with the language of citizenship and naturalization.

Read the passages that follow until you feel you understand enough to answer the questions that appear in this section. It is best if you read this *aloud* and underline those words that you are unfamiliar with. Look them up either in the Word List at the back of this book or in a dictionary that gives pronunciation. Then work on the practice exercises.

As you read, speak slowly and carefully. It has been my experience that more people fail the naturalization examination because the examiner does not understand the applicant than because the applicant does not know the answer. If you are having difficulties pronouncing certain words, review the section on Pronunciation Practice in the Appendix. Practice makes perfect! You know you are working to get something that is important to you and your family, so do your best on the next section of this book.

Like the Pretest, this section will show you what you need to practice. Do the short exercise below for writing practice.

Print your full name here _____

Your address _____
       House number first   Zip Code

The date here _____

Your Permanent Resident Card number here _____

In your own words, write the answer to the question: How can I go from alien to citizen?

_____

_____

_____

_____

_____

_____

_____

Check your answer with the information on page 20.

Practice Test of Written English

Test yourself on the requirements for naturalization by answering the questions in the spaces provided. This test will help you measure your progress. If you do well, continue to the next practice test. If you get several items wrong, review Part One.

To become a naturalized citizen of the United States:

1. How old must you be? _____

_____

2. Do you have to be lawfully admitted to the United States? _____

_____

3. Is there any residence requirement for naturalization? _____

_____

4. Do you have to be able to speak English? _____

_____

5. Do you have to be able to read and write English?_____

_____

6. Do you have to be of good moral character? _____

_____

7. Do you need to know some American history?_____

_____

8. Do you need to know what the Constitution is and how it protects you? _____

_____

9. Do you need to know how the government of the United States functions? _____

_____

10. Is there any exception to the requirement that you know the fundamentals of American history and government?_____

_____

Check your answers to these questions with the answer key on pages 170–171. If you have answered all of the preceding questions correctly, answer the next set of questions in the spaces provided. Otherwise, go back and review the sections of the book that pertain to the questions you did not know.

11. What is the first step in becoming a citizen of the United States? _

_____

12. What is meant by being lawfully admitted to this country?_____

_____

13. Why must you be very careful in filling out Form N-400? _____

_____

14. If you wish to change your name, may you do so?_____

_____

If your answers agree with the answer key on page 171, continue on to the next questions. If not, go back and review the sections of the book that pertain to the questions you did not know.

15. What rights do citizens have that immigrants do not have? _____

_____

16. What is another name for an immigrant?_____

_____

17. Do immigrants live under the laws and Constitution of the United States? _____

_____

18. Can every person who enters the United States become a citizen? Explain. _____

_____

19. Is every citizen a voter? Explain. _____

_____

If your answers are correct (see the answer key on page 171), continue on to the next questions. If not, go back and review the sections of the book that pertain to the questions you did not know.

20. When can an immigrant file a petition for naturalization? _____

_____

21. Is any investigation of the applicant made before he or she becomes a citizen? _____

_____

22. Does the applicant have to take any test? _____

_____

23. Will this be difficult or easy? Explain. _____

_____

24. Is there anything special to be done at the interview? _____

_____

If your answers are correct (see the answer key on page 171), fill in the blanks next to the questions. If not, go back and review the sections of the book that pertain to the questions you did not know.

25. The name of the governor of the state where I live is _____

_____

26. The two senators from this state are _____

and_____.

27. I live in the_____Congressional District.

28. The name of my representative is _____.

29. I want to become a citizen of the United States because_____

_____

30. I think it is important for a citizen to vote because _____

_____

One of the requirements for naturalization is "good moral character." See if you can describe good moral character in the space provided. Be as specific as you can.

31. What is meant by good moral character? _____

_____

_____

_____

_____

_____

_____

_____

_____

Note that you must locate the answers to questions 25–30 yourself. The answer to question 31 may be found in Reading Practice I.

How many answers did you have correct in this Practice Test? Put the number here:_____

Reading Practice I

Practice your oral English by reading this passage aloud.

Good Moral Character

In general, good moral character means that you act in accordance with society's principles of right or good conduct and that you are honest and ethical. The USCIS has given the following examples of things that might show a lack of good moral character:

- Illegal gambling
- Terrorist acts
- Drug or alcohol addiction
- Prostitution
- Criminal record during period of residence here or conviction for murder at any time
- Lying under oath in order to gain citizenship
- Polygamy (having more than one spouse at the same time)
- Failing to pay court-ordered child support or alimony payments
- Persecuting anyone because of race, religion, national origin, political opinion, or social group

It is important to answer all questions relating to this subject truthfully! If you do not tell the truth, the USCIS may deny your application.

It is important to note that if you have committed certain serious crimes, USCIS may decide to remove you from the United States. If you have questions, you may want to seek advice from an immigrant assistance organization or an immigration attorney before applying.

Except for the crimes of murder and aggravated felony, the requirement of good moral character refers to the immigrant's behavior during his or her period of residence here. If your answer to question 31 was similar to the following, it indicates that you understand what is acceptable behavior (action) and what is not acceptable.

Good moral character means that you know the difference between right and wrong, that you choose to obey the laws of the United States and to observe the standards of your new country.

HOW ARE YOU DOING?

Read each question aloud. Answer by writing "yes" or "no" on the line next to the question.

1. Have you at any time, anywhere, ever ordered, incited, assisted, or otherwise participated in the persecution of any person because of race, religion, national origin, or political opinion? _____

_____

2. Have you ever failed to comply with the Selective Service laws? __

_____

3. Since becoming a permanent resident, have you ever failed to file a Federal income tax return? _____

_____

4. Do you believe in the Constitution and form of government of the United States? _____

_____

5. Have you ever given false testimony for the purpose of obtaining any immigration benefit? _____

_____

Did you understand the questions?

Did you answer "no" to questions 1, 2, 3, and 5?

Did you answer "yes" to question 4?

You passed the test.

Practice saying these words:

assist   **service**   **participate**
persecute   **allegiance**

Look them up in the Word List.

Reading Practice II

Now test your progress in oral English by reading and answering the questions following the reading passages. Read aloud in front of a mirror or have someone listen to your pronunciation.

Who Can Be Naturalized?

Men and women who have entered the United States for permanent residence, or who have qualified for amnesty under the terms of the 1986 Immigration Reform and Control Act, and who want to be citizens may apply for naturalization. Others have done it, and you can do it, too!

When we move from alien to citizen, we become equal to people who were born here or who were naturalized before us. No one asks how or when! We can start the process if we are 18 years or older, were legally accepted for permanent residence, and have lived here for five or more years. There are some exceptions to the residence requirement; and I know they are based on the immigration laws.

The first step to naturalization is to obtain and fill out an Application for Naturalization (Form N-400) and then mail it with a check or money order for $390 (which includes the fingerprinting fee) to the appropriate regional office of the USCIS. And then wait!

REVIEW

1. What do the following words mean?

amnesty	eligible	naturalization
application	exception	newcomer
apply	ineligible	requirement
basis	lawfully	residence
eligibility	legally	resident

How did you do?
Check your answers with the Word List at the back of this book.

2. Use each of the above words in a sentence.

For example: The *basis* for my *eligibility* is five years as a permanent *resident* of the United States.

Here, three words were used in the same sentence. Can you do the same? If you have difficulty, go back to Part One to find how the words were used there.

_____

_____

_____

_____

_____

_____

_____

_____

_____

_____

_____

Writing Practice

Write the following sentences, completing those that have blanks for answer choices.

1. I want to be an American citizen. _____
   _____

2. I have studied the American Constitution. _____
   _____

3. I have a pen in my right hand. _____
   _____

4. Today is a beautiful day. _____
   _____

5. This pen has _____ (*blue, black*) ink. _____
   _____

6. I went to a citizenship school for two months. _____
   _____

7. There are three colors in our flag: red, white, and blue. _____
   _____

8. There are fifty (50) states in the United States. _____
   _____

9. I came to _____ (*state*) from _____ (*country*)
   on _____ (*April 5th*) (*yesterday*) (*last week*). _____
   _____
   _____

10. I am wearing a _____ (*blue, red, green*) dress. _____
    _____

11. I am here to take my test today. _____
    _____

12. Yesterday was a (*cold, warm, hot*) day. _____
    _____

13. I can read, write, and speak simple English. _____

_____

14. There are many cars on the street._____

_____

15. I am working at _____. _____

_____

16. I am wearing _____ (*black, brown, gray*) shoes._____

_____

17. It is raining now. _____

_____

18. I have been married for ___ years. _____

_____

19. We do not have any children (yet). _____

_____

20. We have ____ children: ____ sons and ____ daughters._____

_____

21. We have ____ son(s)._____

_____

22. My first name is _____. _____

_____

23. I was married ____ years ago. _____

_____

24. May I write something else? _____

_____

25. I will do my best to be a worthy citizen. _____

_____

26. I enjoy my work. _____

_____

Review: More Writing Practice

Read each question carefully. Then write your answers in the spaces provided. Read your answer out loud to see if it makes sense. You can check what you wrote with the answers on the next page.

1. In your own words, write the answer to the question "What is naturalization?" _____

_____

_____

2. In your own words, write the answer to the question "Why is it important for me to go through the naturalization process?" _____

_____

_____

_____

_____

_____

_____

_____

Now turn the book upside down and compare your answers with the answers given below. If you left something out, write the answer again, either below this sentence, or on another sheet of paper. If you wrote the answer using different words, you may still be correct. However, the main meaning of these answers must be the same. If not, write both question and correct answer on a separate sheet of paper.

ACCEPTABLE ANSWERS

1. Naturalization is the process of becoming a citizen, or the act of going from *alien to citizen.*

2. I want to be able to *vote.* I also think it is important to get an American *passport,* and to help some of my relatives come into the United States of America so our family is not separated. It may also enable me to apply for a government job or to *be elected* to public office. And it will not be necessary for me to show a *card* to prove that I belong here!

Step 4—Serious Study—History and Civics

Part One included the *main requirements* for naturalization. There are also two *educational requirements* for naturalization.

The *first educational requirement* is that you understand English and be able to read, write, and speak words in ordinary use. Remember: Only those persons who are physically unable to do this, or persons over 50 years old who have lived in the United States as permanent residents for over 20 years, or who are over 55 with more than 15 years of residence, are excused from this requirement. You have already had practice in reading and writing words needed to meet this educational requirement.

Now, you will also learn the facts that you need in order to meet the *second educational requirement* for naturalization: to demonstrate a knowledge and understanding of the history, principles, and form of government of the United States (civics). An applicant who has a physical or developmental disability or a mental impairment may be exempt from this requirement.

Note: This is a self-help book. While you are learning important facts, each unit aims to help you improve your English. Pay attention to words and their meaning while you read and learn the content in this section. You will learn all you need to know—and much more!

Our Government

Our government is a **democracy.** That means it is a government of the people, by the people, and for the people. It is a government by the elected representatives of all the voters. It is a *tripartite* government, which means it has three parts, or branches.

Our government is also a **republic.** This means that the supreme power is given to representatives elected by popular vote of all citizens.

You see that democracy and republic mean almost the same thing. Long ago, in small units of government, citizens got together and made the laws for their communities. That is the real meaning of democracy. Today that kind of democracy exists only in a few small towns in the northeastern part of our country. Through town meetings, all of the voters decide on what is to be done in their town.

Of course, this is not possible where a great many people live. Today, we make our voices heard by voting for people to represent us. The two largest political parties in the United States, the Democratic and the Republican parties, derive their names from *democracy* and *republic;* so it should not be difficult to remember these words.

Our country is a **federation,** or association, of states. The government for the whole country is, therefore, called the *federal government*. The plan for this government is set by the Constitution, the supreme law of our land.

Remember: The government is divided into three branches—the legislative, the executive, and the judicial. That is why it is called a *tripartite* government.

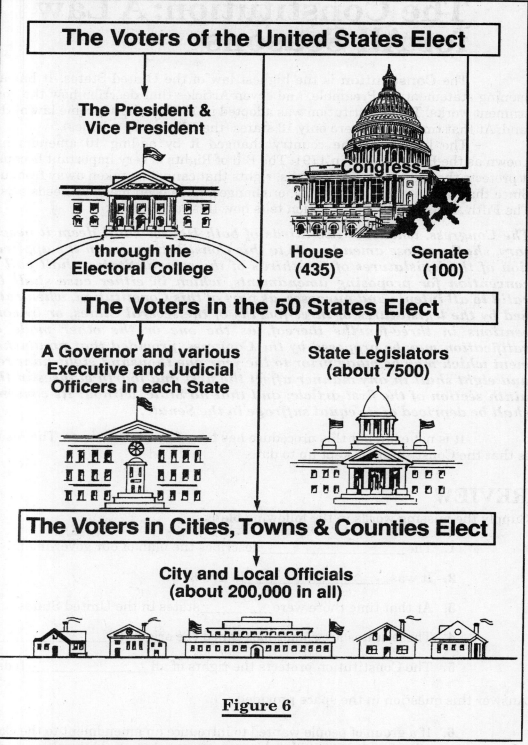

The Voters of the United States Elect

The President &
Vice President

through the
Electoral College

Congress

House
(435)

Senate
(100)

The Voters in the 50 States Elect

A Governor and various
Executive and Judicial
Officers in each State

State Legislators
(about 7500)

The Voters in Cities, Towns & Counties Elect

City and Local Officials
(about 200,000 in all)

Figure 6

Source: U.S. Department of Justice, Immigration and Naturalization Service

The Constitution: A Law for All Seasons

The **Constitution** is the highest law of the United States. It has an opening statement, or Preamble, and seven Articles that describe how the government works. The Constitution was adopted in 1789 as the supreme law of the land. At that time, there were only 13 states (the 13 original colonies).

The leaders of the country changed it by adding 10 amendments known as the Bill of Rights in 1791. The Bill of Rights is very important because it protects the rights of all Americans, rights that cannot be taken away from us. Since that time other amendments, or changes, have been made as needs arise. The Fifth Article of the Constitution tells how this can be done:

The Congress, whenever two-thirds of both Houses shall deem it necessary, shall propose amendments to this Constitution, or, on the application of the legislatures of two-thirds of the several States, shall call a convention for proposing amendments, which in either case shall be valid to all intents and purposes, as part of this Constitution, when ratified by the legislatures of three-fourths of the several States, or by conventions in three-fourths thereof, as the one or the other mode of ratification may be proposed by the Congress; provided that no amendment which may be made prior to the year one thousand eight hundred and eight shall in any manner affect the first and fourth clauses in the ninth section of the first article; and that no State, without its consent, shall be deprived of its equal suffrage in the Senate.

It is not easy, but this procedure has been followed 27 times. The result is that the Constitution is kept up to date.

REVIEW

Supply the missing words in the following blanks.

1. The_____describes the plan of our government.

2. It was_____in 1789.

3. At that time there were_____states in the United States.

4. These states are sometimes called the original _____.

5. The Constitution protects the rights of all_____today.

Answer this question in the space provided.

6. If a group of people wanted to introduce an amendment to the Constitution making it illegal to carry guns, what would they have to do?

_____

_____

_____

See the answer key on page 172.

THE CONSTITUTION AS IT WAS ADOPTED

Preamble (Introduction)
Explains the purposes of the people in adopting the Constitution.

First Article
Provides for a Congress and defines its power to make laws.

Second Article
Provides for the election of a President and Vice President, with
defined powers, and for the *appointment* of other officials.

Third Article
Sets up a Supreme Court, authorizes the Congress to set up
other courts, and defines their powers.

Fourth Article
Defines relationships between the Federal Government and the States,
and between the States themselves.

Fifth Article
Tells how the Constitution may be amended.

Sixth Article
Accepts responsibility for all debts that the Nation owed before the adoption
of the Constitution; declares that the Constitution, constitutional laws, and
treaties are the supreme law of the land; and provides that all public
officers must take an oath to support the Constitution.

Seventh Article
Declares that ratification (approval) by nine States will
put the Constitution into effect.

Figure 7

Source: U.S. Department of Justice, Immigration and Naturalization Service

THE BILL OF RIGHTS—1791

First Amendment

Forbids the Congress to interfere with religion, free speech, a free press, or with the right to *assemble* peaceably, or to petition the Government.

Second Amendment

Guarantees to the people the right to have weapons.

Third Amendment

Guarantees against lodging soldiers in private houses without the *consent* of the owners.

Fourth Amendment

Provides that there shall be no search or *seizure* of persons, houses, goods, or papers, without a *warrant.*

Fifth Amendment

Declares that there shall be no *trial* for serious offenses without a *grand jury indictment,* no repeated trials for the same offense, no *condemnation* without trial, no compulsion to be a *witness* against oneself, and no property taken for public use except at a fair price.

Sixth Amendment

Requires a speedy and public trial for criminal offenses in the district where the crime was committed, a fair jury, a plain statement of the *accusation,* gives the *accused* the right to be represented by a lawyer and to *compel* the attendance of his witnesses, and requires all witnesses to *testify* in the presence of the accused.

Seventh Amendment

Provides that in *lawsuits* about anything valued at more than $20, a trial by jury shall be allowed.

Eighth Amendment

Prohibits too large *bail* or *fines,* and cruel or unusual *punishments.*

Ninth Amendment

Declares that rights not stated in the Constitution are not therefore taken away from the people.

Tenth Amendment

States that powers not delegated to the United States nor prohibited by the Constitution to the States are reserved to the States or to the people.

Figure 8

Source: U.S. Department of Justice, Immigration and Naturalization Service

AMENDMENTS PASSED AFTER THE BILL OF RIGHTS

Eleventh Amendment (1795)
A citizen of one state, or an alien, cannot sue another state in a Federal court.

Twelfth Amendment (1804)
Electors must vote for President and Vice President separately.

Thirteenth Amendment (1865)
Ended slavery.

Fourteenth Amendment (1868)
All persons born or naturalized in the United States are citizens.

Fifteenth Amendment (1870)
No person can be kept from voting because of race or color.

Sixteenth Amendment (1913)
Congress has the power to put a tax on money earned by the people.

Seventeenth Amendment (1913)
Senators are to be elected by the people.

Eighteenth Amendment (1919)
Prohibited the making, selling or transportation of intoxicating liquor.

Nineteenth Amendment (1920)
No person can be kept from voting because of being a woman.

Twentieth Amendment (1933)
The President, the Vice President, and the Congress shall take office in January.

Twenty-first Amendment (1933)
Did away with the Eighteenth Amendment.

Twenty-second Amendment (1951)
The same person cannot be elected President more than twice.

Twenty-third Amendment (1961)
Citizens living in the District of Columbia can vote for
President and Vice President.

Twenty-fourth Amendment (1964)
Citizens cannot be made to pay a tax to vote for the President,
the Vice President or members of the Congress.

Twenty-fifth Amendment (1967)
The Vice President becomes Acting President when the President is disabled.

Twenty-sixth Amendment (1971)
A citizen shall not be denied the right to vote because of age
if he is eighteen years of age or older.

Twenty-seventh Amendment (1992)
Compensation for the services of Senators and Representatives
shall not be changed until an election is held.

Figure 9

Source: U.S. Department of Justice, Immigration and Naturalization Service

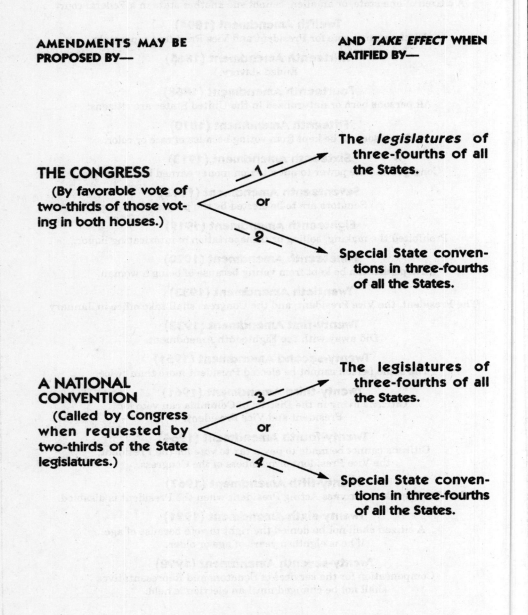

FOUR WAYS OF AMENDING OUR
FEDERAL CONSTITUTION

**AMENDMENTS MAY BE
PROPOSED BY—**

**AND *TAKE EFFECT* WHEN
RATIFIED BY—**

THE CONGRESS
(By favorable vote of
two-thirds of those vot-
ing in both houses.)

_1_ or _2_

The *legislatures* of
three-fourths of all
the States.

Special State conven-
tions in three-fourths
of all the States.

**A NATIONAL
CONVENTION**
(Called by Congress
when requested by
two-thirds of the State
legislatures.)

_3_ or _4_

The legislatures of
three-fourths of all
the States.

Special State conven-
tions in three-fourths
of all the States.

<u>**Figure 10**</u>

Source: U.S. Department of Justice, Immigration and Naturalization Service

70

Reading Practice

Practice your oral English by reading the passage below. Then check your understanding by writing about what you have read in the spaces provided.

The Government of the United States

The government of the United States of America is a democracy, a government of the people, by the people, and for the people. It is a tripartite government because it has three parts, or branches. (*Tri* means three.) You know that a triangle has three sides. In the same way, our government has three branches.

These branches are the legislative, or law-making, the executive, and the judicial. The executive branch carries out the laws. The judicial branch judges laws.

The plan of our government is in the Constitution, the highest law of the land. When the Constitution was first written, the leaders of the new country left out the rights of the people. This was an oversight for the citizens wanting a guarantee that their rights would be protected. And so, the first 10 amendments to the Constitution were adopted to do just that. They are called the Bill of Rights.

These rights are listed on page 68. Read them again! Then write a summary of them in your own words on the lines below. Check to see how your summary agrees with paragraph number three on page 72.

_____

_____

_____

_____

_____

_____

_____

_____

_____

Summary: How the Bill of Rights Protects Americans

1. The first 10 amendments to the Constitution are called the Bill of Rights.

2. These rights are guaranteed by the Constitution, the highest law of our land, and are protected by the Supreme Court, the highest court of our land. The amendments were adopted in 1791 and now are over 200 years old. They are still used to protect us.

3. These amendments include: freedom of religion, of speech, and of the press; the right to assemble peacefully and to petition (ask) the government to set right or cancel a law that denies them their rights. The Bill of Rights also guarantees that no one will come into your house to search it without a warrant. And we have the right to bear arms (carry guns) to protect ourselves, as well as the right to a fair trial if we are accused of a crime. The last amendment, the 10th, states that any power not given to the federal government is a power of the state or the people. (We will read more about this in the section on state and local governments.)

4. Sometimes, we hear of a witness in a court trial, "taking the Fifth." This refers to the Fifth Amendment, "no person shall be compelled to be a witness against himself, nor be deprived of life, liberty or property without due process of law."

5. Another important guarantee of "due process" is in the Fourteenth Amendment, which was adopted in 1868 after the Civil War. The Fourteenth Amendment also tells us the meaning of the word citizen:

"All persons born or naturalized in the United States, and subject to its jurisdiction [authority] are citizens of the United States, and of the state where they reside..."

PRACTICE

Answer these questions in your own words.

1. Why is it important that the rights of all the people are protected?

_____

_____

Check your answer with the summary above.

2. What is meant by due process of law? _____

_____

_____

Check your answer with the Word List at the back of this book.

The Federal Government: Form and Structure

The Constitution broadly outlines the form and structure of the federal government. Details of operation and management have been worked out over the years since 1789, so that what we have today is a workable system of government for 50 states.

The writers of the Constitution set up the government in such a way that no person, or group of persons, would have too much power. Our system of government is based on two principles: the *separation of powers* and a system of *checks and balances*. Let us see what these principles mean.

The government is divided into three branches—the legislative, the executive, and the judicial—each with separate functions.

The **legislative branch,** or **Congress,** makes the laws. It is composed of a Senate and a House of Representatives. Two senators are elected from each state, each for a six-year term; representatives are elected for terms of two years. The number of representatives each state has is determined by the size of its population.

The **executive branch** is headed by the president, who is elected for a term of four years. A vice president is elected at the same time and from the same political party. The Constitution tells how a president may be removed from office. It provides that upon such removal or upon the death of the president, the vice president takes office. If the vice president is also removed from office, or dies, the Speaker of the House of Representatives would take office as president of the United States.

The third branch of the federal government is the judicial branch. Its function is to interpret the laws. To do this, there is a network of federal courts, the highest of which is the Supreme Court.

Briefly, this explains the **separation of powers.** Now let us see how the **system of checks and balances** works.

Each of the three branches of government has been set up to check the other branches. For example, the president must sign into law all bills passed by Congress; if he thinks that a bill is not good, he can veto or say no to that bill. Then the bill must go back to Congress. It can only be passed by a two-thirds vote of both houses of Congress after the president's veto.

The president appoints many high government officials, his cabinet, head of agencies, and federal judges (even those of the Supreme Court). But all of these appointments must be approved by the Senate. This is one way the legislative branch checks the executive branch.

In this process, the judicial branch has the "last word" over the other two branches. The Supreme Court may decide that a law made by Congress and signed by the president is unconstitutional; that is, it is not in accordance with the Constitution. There is no appeal from a decision of the Supreme Court!

REVIEW

Do you know what these words mean? Write the meaning next to the word. If you are not sure, look up the meaning in the Word List at the end of the book.

1. judicial_____

2. interpret _____

3. Senate _____

4. House of Representatives _____

5. separation of powers _____

6. system of checks and balances _____

7. legislative_____

8. executive_____

From the list of new words in items 1–8, choose the words that fit in the blanks in sentences 9–13.

9. Two principles on which our government is based are_____

    and _____.

10. The _____ branch is made up of two houses,

    the _____ and the _____.

11. The _____ branch carries out the laws.

12. If the president dies or is unable to perform his duties, the _____

    _____ becomes president.

13. The _____ branch, made up of a series of courts,

    _____ the law.

See the answer key on page 172.

Congress: Your Representatives

The legislative branch of the federal government is called the **Congress,** which, according to the Constitution, has power to make laws for the nation. The Constitution also sets the qualifications for senators and representatives and tells how they are to be elected.

At the present time, there are **100 senators (two from each of the 50 states) and 435 representatives apportioned according to population.** In the Senate both of the senators from your state represent you, but in the House of Representatives only the representative from the district where you live represents you.

The function of Congress is to make laws, but nowhere in the Constitution is there a statement of the exact steps that must be taken in the law-making process. The steps by which a bill introduced by a senator or a representative becomes a law have developed over the years. In fact, the whole committee system, so important in the law-making process, was set up by Congress in order to handle its business more efficiently.

A Tripartite System

The Principle of Checks and Balances in Our Government

(Examples are shown below)

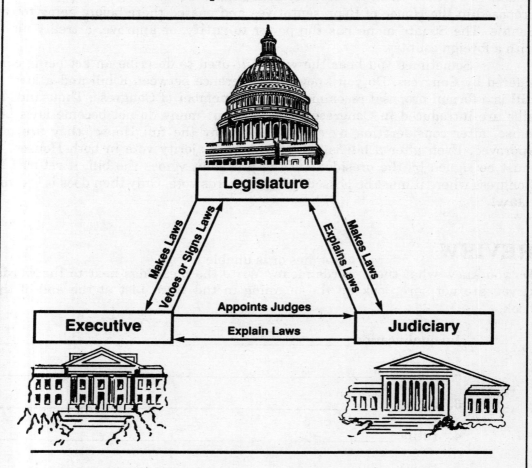

Legislature

Makes Laws

Vetoes or Signs Laws

Makes Laws

Explains Laws

Appoints Judges

Executive

Explain Laws

Judiciary

This chart indicates one way in which each branch of our Federal Government is authorized to check (to hold back, to slow up, and even to change) the action of each of the other two branches.

<u>**Figure 11**</u>

Source: U.S. Department of Justice, Immigration and Naturalization Service

Congress begins its sessions on January 3 of each year and is in session until the members of both Houses vote to **adjourn,** or close, the meeting. Each of the Houses has its own chairperson: The vice president presides over the Senate; the speaker of the House of Representatives is chosen by the members of that body and presides over all of its sessions.

Congress has many important powers: to coin money, to set taxes and collect them, to declare war, and (a very important power to you) to establish the requirements for naturalization. It has many other powers, and each of the Houses has some special powers: for example, all bills relating to money must be proposed in the House of Representatives and passed there before going to the Senate. The Senate alone has the power to **ratify,** or approve, a treaty made with a foreign country.

Sometimes you hear the word *bill* used to describe an act being considered by Congress. Do you know the difference between a bill and a law? A **bill** is a formal proposal recommended by a member of Congress. Thousands of bills are introduced in Congress each year, but many do not become laws because, after consideration by committees or by the full House, they are not approved. Even after a bill is approved by a majority vote in both Houses, it must be signed by the president. If the president vetoes the bill, it returns to Congress where it must be passed by a two-thirds vote. Only then does it become a **law!**

REVIEW

Do you know what these words mean? Write the meanings next to the words. If you are not sure, look up the meaning in the Word List at the end of the book.

1. qualification _____

2. apportion _____

3. adjourn _____

4. ratify _____

5. treaty _____

6. majority _____

Now, write the answers to the following questions in the space provided.

7. Why does the Congress have two houses? _____

_____

8. Can you introduce a bill in Congress? _____

_____

9. When does Congress begin each session? _____

_____

HOW A BILL BECOMES A LAW

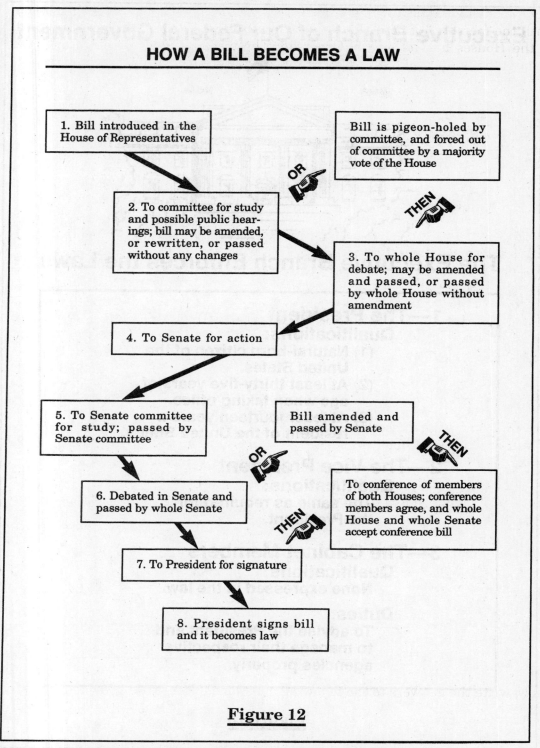

1. Bill introduced in the House of Representatives

Bill is pigeon-holed by committee, and forced out of committee by a majority vote of the House

OR

THEN

2. To committee for study and possible public hearings; bill may be amended, or rewritten, or passed without any changes

3. To whole House for debate; may be amended and passed, or passed by whole House without amendment

4. To Senate for action

5. To Senate committee for study; passed by Senate committee

Bill amended and passed by Senate

OR

THEN

6. Debated in Senate and passed by whole Senate

To conference of members of both Houses; conference members agree, and whole House and whole Senate accept conference bill

THEN

7. To President for signature

8. President signs bill and it becomes law

Figure 12

Source: U.S. Department of Justice, Immigration and Naturalization Service

Executive Branch of Our Federal Government

The Executive Branch Enforces the Laws

1—The President
  Qualifications:
      (1) Natural-born citizen of the United States.
      (2) At least thirty-five years of age when taking office.
      (3) At least fourteen years a resident of the United States.

2—The Vice President
  Qualifications:
      The same as required for the President.

3—The Cabinet Members
  Qualifications:
      None expressed in the law.

  Duties:
      To advise the President and to manage their respective agencies properly.

Figure 13

Source: U.S. Department of Justice, Immigration and Naturalization Service

The President

Term of office—4 years.
Salary—$400,000 a year.
Election—November of every fourth year.
Inauguration—January 20 following election.
Elected—By the people through the Electoral College.
Qualifications—Natural-born citizen at least 35 years old
and at least 14 years a resident of the United States.

Succession to the office—(People next in line to be
president if the president cannot carry out his or her
duties.)
1. Vice President.
2. Speaker of the House of Representatives.
3. President pro tempore of the Senate.
4. Secretary of State.
5. Secretary of the Treasury.
6. Secretary of Defense.
7. Attorney General.
8. Secretary of the Interior.
9. Secretary of Agriculture.
10. Secretary of Commerce.
11. Secretary of Labor.
12. Secretary of Health and Human Services.
13. Secretary of Homeland Security.
14. Secretary of Housing and Urban Development.
15. Secretary of Transportation.
16. Secretary of Energy.
17. Secretary of Education.
18. Secretary of Veterans' Affairs.

Chief power and duty—To enforce the Constitution, the
laws made by the Congress, and treaties.

Other powers—
1. To veto bills.
2. To recommend bills to the Congress.
3. To call special sessions of the Congress.
4. To deliver messages to the Congress.
5. To appoint Federal judges.
6. To appoint representatives to foreign countries.
7. To appoint Department heads and other important
officials.
8. To pardon.
9. To carry on official business with foreign nations.
10. To be Commander-in-Chief of the Armed Forces.

Figure 14

Source: U.S. Department of Justice, Immigration and Naturalization Service

10. When does Congress adjourn? _____

_____

11. How does a bill become a law? _____

_____

Note the following paragraph.

An English writer once said that the men who founded the United States had a clear idea of what they wanted to put into the Constitution and then left it to later generations to work out the details. He added that this plan has been remarkably successful.

12. In your own words, write one example of this.

_____

_____

_____

See the answer key on page 172.

The Presidency

The president is the **chief executive,** or head, of the federal government. His job is to carry out the laws and to manage the affairs of the country. Only the president and the vice president can be voted for by all the citizens of the United States. Both are elected for terms of four years and cannot serve for more than two terms, as provided in Amendment 22 of the Constitution.

The president and his family live in the White House, at 1600 Pennsylvania Avenue, Washington, D.C., a building that symbolizes the dignity of the office. The president also has his office here. If you write a letter to the president, you should address him as Mr. President.

The president takes the oath of office on January 20 following his election. Just as your Oath of Allegiance will be administered by a judge when you become a citizen, the president's oath is administered by a judge—the highest ranking judge in the country, the **Chief Justice of the Supreme Court.**

Here is the oath that the president takes.

PRESIDENTIAL OATH OF OFFICE

I do solemnly swear that I will faithfully execute the office of President of the United States, and will to the best of my ability, preserve, protect and defend the Constitution of the United States.

Because the president has many important responsibilities, he appoints people to help him. These people, each heading an executive department, make up the cabinet. All cabinet members must be approved by the Senate before they can serve. Remember, this is part of our system of checks and balances! Following are the cabinet members and their duties:

Position	Duties
Attorney General	heads the Department of Justice (including the Immigration and Naturalization Service) and represents the government in all legal matters.
Secretary of Agriculture	manages farming and the improvement of conditions among farmers.
Secretary of Commerce	manages trade relations between the U.S. and other countries and helps business people.
Secretary of Defense	manages the armed services (Army, Navy, Air Force, and Marines).
Secretary of Education	supervises special programs of education authorized by the Congress.
Secretary of Energy	coordinates the work of agencies relating to the development of power.
Secretary of Health and Human Services	is in charge of the common needs of the people, including social security, child labor, and public health and assistance.
Secretary of Homeland Security	coordinates border and transportation security, protects critical infrastructure, and provides protection from chemical and biological threats. Heads U.S. Citizenship and Immigration Services (USCIS).
Secretary of Housing and Urban Development	handles the financing and construction of public housing.
Secretary of the Interior	takes care of all public lands.
Secretary of Labor	manages the conditions of working people.
Secretary of State	has charge of all foreign affairs.
Secretary of Transportation	coordinates different kinds of transportation: aviation, highways, railroads, and so on.
Secretary of the Treasury	has charge of federal funds and taxes.
Secretary of Veterans' Affairs	oversees programs and advises president.

Now you know what heavy responsibilities may rest with the president and his advisers (the cabinet).

What about the vice president? As you may remember, he presides over the Senate at all of its sessions. That is an important responsibility. But probably the vice president's most important duty is to become president if the president dies, resigns, or is removed from office.

The first president of the United States was George Washington. His birthday, in February, is a national holiday. George Washington commanded the army during the American Revolution and brought a group of inexperienced, poorly equipped soldiers to victory. When the Constitution was written, it provided that one of the duties of the president was to be commander-in-chief of the armed forces.

Another president whose birthday is a holiday, at least in some parts of the country, is Abraham Lincoln, who served during the Civil War and who is credited with saving the Union and freeing the slaves with the Emancipation Proclamation.

REVIEW

Do you know what these words mean? Write the meanings next to the words. If you are not sure, look up the meaning in the Word List at the end of the book.

1. chief executive _____

2. oath _____

3. commerce _____

4. energy _____

5. treasury _____

6. cabinet _____

7. agriculture _____

8. urban _____

9. attorney _____

Now write the answers to the following questions in the space provided.

10. Is the president's most important duty to make the laws or to carry them out? _____

_____

11. Does the president have many responsibilities or a few responsibilities? _____

_____

12. Who helps the president? _____

_____

13. Can a naturalized citizen become president of the United States?

_____

14. What oath does the president take? When does he take it? _____

_____

See the answer key on page 172.

The Court System

The **judicial branch** of the government is responsible for interpreting the laws. The Constitution calls for one Supreme Court and "such inferior [lower] courts as the Congress shall from time to time ordain and establish." Congress has set up a series of lower federal courts that have the right to hear and decide cases under federal laws. This system of courts includes district courts, courts of appeal, and finally the **Supreme Court,** the highest court of the country. Once the Supreme Court has made a decision, that is the last word. There can be no further appeal.

There are nine judges on the Supreme Court, all appointed by the president for life. When a case comes before the Supreme Court, the justices hear it together. The decision is reached by majority vote. Sometimes, justices who disagree, or **dissent,** write minority or dissenting opinions. But the majority vote is final.

At one time, the Supreme Court justices were referred to as the "nine old men" but that is no longer appropriate, since in 1981 the first woman justice, Sandra Day O'Connor, was appointed to the Supreme Court.

The lower federal courts have jurisdiction, or authority, in disputes over government security, immigration, national banks, shipping on the high seas, and other matters. Cases that most of us are involved in are decided at the state or local level. Each state has a network of courts in which persons who have broken state laws are tried. Each city also has courts in which cases involving local laws are tried.

REVIEW

Do you know what these words mean? Write the meanings next to the words. If you are not sure, look up the meaning in the Word List at the end of the book.

1. appeal _____

2. dispute_____

3. jurisdiction _____

4. dissent (dissenting)_____

Now, write the answers to the following questions in the space provided.

5. What is the function of the judicial branch of the government? ___

_____

6. What is the highest court in the United States?_____

_____

7. How is this court set up?_____

_____

Judicial Branch of Our Federal Government
The Courts Explain the Laws

The Supreme Court is the Highest Court in the Land

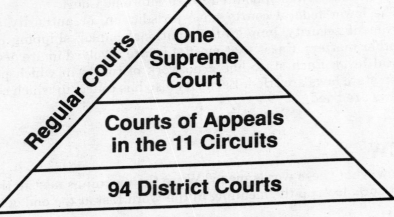

Regular Courts

- One Supreme Court
- Courts of Appeals in the 11 Circuits
- 94 District Courts

Special Courts

One Court of Claims (1855)	One Court of Customs (1926)	One Court of Customs and Patent Appeals	Court of Military Appeals

"Equal Justice Under Law"

Figure 15

S. Department of Justice, Immigration and Naturalization Service

8. Who is presently the chief justice? _____

_____

9. Are there any courts other than federal courts? _____

_____

Match the first part of each sentence (column A) with the letter in column B in order to make a complete thought. (Choices may be repeated.)

COLUMN A	COLUMN B
10. _____ Disputes under federal laws	a. that a law is unconstitutional.
11. _____ Naturalization procedures	b. related to shipping on the high sea.
12. _____ The Supreme Court can decide	c. are handled by federal courts.
13. _____ Violations of local law	d. are handled by local courts.

See the answer key on page 172.

State and Local Governments

State Government

When you apply for naturalization, you must prove that you have lived for at least three months in the state from which you apply. You should know the names of the governor and the two senators from your state.

Each of the 50 states has three branches of government—legislative, executive, judicial—just like the U.S. federal government, but not all of them function in the same way. The reason that different patterns emerged is because the 13 original colonies had governments before the U.S. Constitution was ratified in 1789. The first to have its own constitution was New Hampshire. In fact, if you visit New Hampshire today, you will see the nation's oldest state legislature still functioning in its original chambers.

Like Congress, the state legislatures make laws for the state, but they cannot make laws that affect all Americans. They cannot declare war, regulate post offices, coin money, control trade with foreign countries, or decide who can become American citizens. According to the U.S. Constitution (the Tenth Amendment), the states have those powers that are not granted to the federal government and that are not specifically denied to them. This gives the states a great deal of power over our everyday lives. Education, health, sanitation, police and fire protection, and voting procedures are some examples of state functions. States impose taxes, even income taxes, regulate businesses that operate within their borders, and perform many functions that protect the lives and property of their residents.

Each state has a chief executive, or governor, elected by the people of the state, who makes sure that the laws are carried out. Like the president, the governor has people to assist and advise him.

The judicial branch of state governments includes a set of courts that have authority to try civil and criminal cases; some states have family and children's courts. All have courts of appeal. All states have correctional departments that regulate jails and prisons within their jurisdiction.

Local Government

Within the states there are smaller subdivisions—counties, cities, towns, and villages—that have governments, too. Laws for their residents are made by bodies often called councils, which have the authority to control streets, traffic, water supply, garbage, parking, and other everyday services. Cities and counties may also impose taxes, such as property and school taxes.

This government has an executive branch too, sometimes headed by a mayor or commissioner, which sees that local laws are enforced. And there is a judicial branch, consisting of municipal courts, traffic courts, and, in some cases, small claims courts. Local governments vary most from state to state. Find out how your local government functions, and when you become a citizen, get involved at this level! It is at this level that residents are in closest contact with their elected officials.

As you learn more about what state and local governments can do, remember that the U.S. Constitution is the supreme law of the land and the Supreme Court can find laws unconstitutional if they go against the Constitution.

REVIEW

Do you know what these words mean? Write the meanings next to the words. If you are not sure, look up the meaning in the Word List at the end of the book.

1. function _____

2. executive _____

3. ratified _____

4. legislative _____

5. legislature _____

6. judicial _____

7. jurisdiction _____

8. unconstitutional _____

Now, write the answers to the following question in the space provided.

9. How does the U.S. Constitution grant rights to the 50 states? ____
_____

See the answer key on page 172.

HOW THE ORGANIZATION OF GOVERNMENT IN CITIES, STATES, AND THE NATION IS MUCH ALIKE

	Each has a Legislative Branch to make laws	Each has an Executive Branch to enforce the laws	Each has a Judicial Branch to explain and apply the laws
The Federal Government:	The Congress. —Senate and House of Representatives.	President, Vice President, 11 Executive Departments, and other executive agencies.	The Federal courts.
The State Government:	The State Legislature. (Two houses in all States but Nebraska.)	The governor and heads of executive departments.	The State courts.
The City Government:	The City Council or Commissioners.	The mayor or manager or board of commissioners.	The city courts.

Figure 16

Source: U.S. Department of Justice, Immigration and Naturalization Service.

87

DELEGATED POWERS IN THE FEDERAL SYSTEM

A. POWERS OF THE FEDERAL GOVERNMENT
(those DELEGATED to it)
EXAMPLES

To control relations with foreign nations.

To punish crimes against the United States.

To establish post offices.

To coin money and regulate its value.

To keep up an army, a navy, and an air corps.

To declare war and make peace.

To set standards for weights and measures.

To regulate commerce among the States and with foreign countries.

To make uniform laws about naturalization and bankruptcy.

To protect authors and inventors by giving copyrights and patents.

To admit new States and to control the territory of the United States.

To make all laws necessary and proper for carrying into effect the expressly stated powers and all othe powers granted by the United States Constitution.

B. CONCURRENT POWERS*
EXAMPLES

To borrow money.

To collect taxes.

To build public works.

To charter banks.

To establish courts.

To help agriculture and industry.

To protect the public health.

C. PROHIBITED POWERS
EXAMPLES

To deny civil rights (such as freedom of speech, press, religion, and assembly).

To pass laws that make illegal something that has already been done legally and honestly.

To pass a law that finds any person guilty without trial.

D. POWERS OF THE STATES (called RESERVED powers)
EXAMPLES

To authorize the establishment of local governments.

To establish and keep up schools.

To regulate city government groups.

To provide for a State militia.

To regulate commerce within the borders of the State.

To regulate labor, industry, and business within the State.

To provide care for orphans and paupers, and for blind, crippled, insane, and other helpless persons.

To make laws on all other subjects not prohibited to the States by the Federal or State Constitutions, and not delegated to the Federal Government.

*Concurrent means belonging to both federal and state governments.

Figure 17

Source: U.S. Department of Justice, Immigration and Naturalization Service

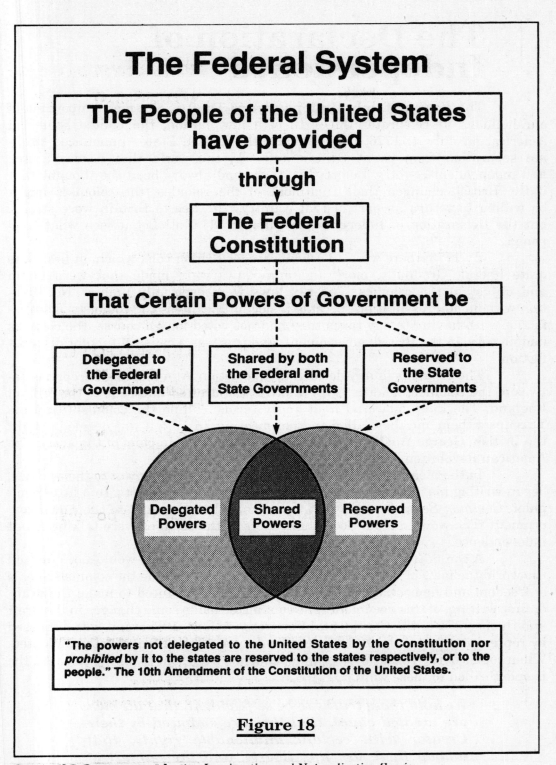

The Federal System

The People of the United States have provided

through

The Federal Constitution

That Certain Powers of Government be

| Delegated to the Federal Government | Shared by both the Federal and State Governments | Reserved to the State Governments |

Delegated Powers | Shared Powers | Reserved Powers

"The powers not delegated to the United States by the Constitution nor *prohibited* by it to the states are reserved to the states respectively, or to the people." The 10th Amendment of the Constitution of the United States.

<u>Figure 18</u>

Source: U.S. Department of Justice, Immigration and Naturalization Service

The Declaration of Independence

The Fourth of July (**Independence Day**) is the most important of our holidays. It celebrates the birth of a new nation, the United States of America, on July 4, 1776. On that date the United States announced its final separation from Great Britain and told the world that it was a free and independent country. Before this, there had always been the thought that if the British changed their treatment of the colonies, the colonists might be willing to return as part of that country. The ties to Britain were strong, but the Declaration of Independence changed all that! Let us see what happened.

By 1773, there were 13 colonies under British rule, which, at first, was quite liberal. Gradually, more and more laws were made that were harsh and unjust to the colonies. The tax laws were especially unfair. "No Taxation without Representation" became a slogan to express the colonists' dissatisfaction with having to pay taxes they had not voted for. Of course, the colonies had no voice in the British government, and this was a cause of further dissatisfaction.

The colonists finally decided to take action. At a meeting of representatives of the colonies, held in 1774, a letter was drafted and sent to the king of England. The king answered it in angry terms, calling the colonists traitors. This upset them and they called another meeting. In 1775 it was decided to fight the British. George Washington was made commander-in-chief of the army. The American Revolution had begun.

In the meantime, Thomas Paine, an English immigrant to the colonies, began writing his ideas about freedom that stirred the colonists. In a little pamphlet, *Common Sense,* he said that the colonies had the right to their own government. The word spread. Soon the leaders of the colonies were talking about independence.

A committee was set up to write a document that would not only tell the world the facts of British injustice but would also include the colonists' ideals of freedom and democracy. Thomas Jefferson was appointed to make the draft, or first writing, of this document. The committee made some changes in the draft and then sent it to the Continental Congress on June 2. There, it was discussed by representatives of the 13 colonies. On July 4, 1776, it was formally adopted. When copies of the Declaration of Independence were sent to all the colonies, the people thrilled to these words.

> *We hold these truths to be self-evident, that all men are created equal, that they are endowed by their Creator with certain unalienable rights, that among these are life, liberty, and the pursuit of happiness. . .*

The whole Declaration appears in the Appendix of this book. Briefly, the Declaration states that governments are set up to protect the rights of the people and that laws can be made only when the people agree to them. That is the basis of democracy.

REVIEW

Do you know what these words mean? Write the meanings next to the words. If you are not sure, look up the meaning in the Word List at the end of the book.

1. traitor_____

2. unalienable_____

3. dissatisfaction _____

4. representation _____

5. slogan_____

6. democracy_____

Now write the answers to the following questions in the blanks provided.

7. No taxation without _____was a popular slogan in the colonies.

8. Rights that belong to us and can never be taken away are____ _____rights.

9. _____has been called a government of the people, by the people, and for the people.

10. The king of England called the colonists _____; a_____is an enemy of the country.

11. By writing to the king, the colonists expressed their_____ with the treatment they had received from the British.

See the answer key on page 172.

THE LIBERTY BELL
"Let Freedom Ring"

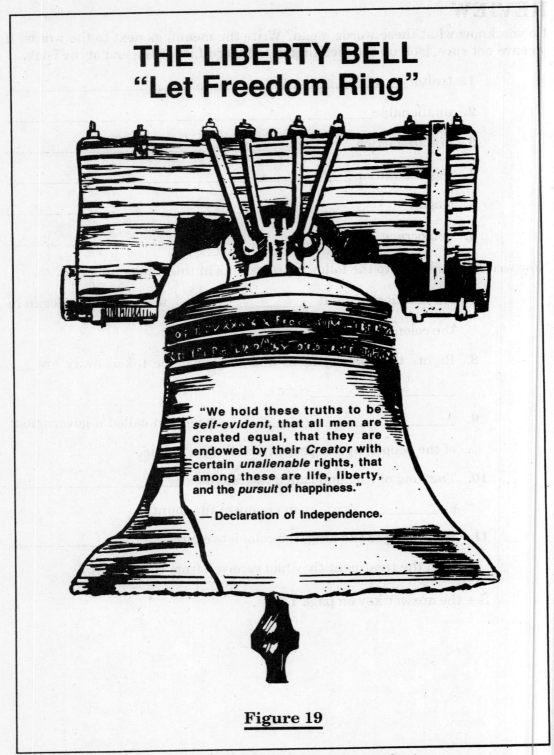

"We hold these truths to be *self-evident*, that all men are created equal, that they are endowed by their *Creator* with certain *unalienable* rights, that among these are life, liberty, and the *pursuit* of happiness."

— Declaration of Independence.

<u>**Figure 19**</u>

Source: U.S. Department of Justice, Immigration and Naturalization Service

The American Flag

The **flag** is a symbol of our country. The colors of the flag have special meanings: RED is for courage; WHITE is for truth; BLUE is for honor. The American national **anthem** is the **"Star-Spangled Banner,"** which refers to the flag. Sometimes the flag is called other names—Old Glory, the Stars and Stripes, the Red, White, and Blue, or just the Colors. Before the American Revolution, most of the colonies used the British flag. But when anger grew at their treatment by Great Britain, the colonists took down that flag and put up their own.

One year after the Declaration of Independence, in 1777, the American flag was officially adopted. It was made by Betsy Ross. The first flag had 13 stripes, to mark the colonies, and 13 stars, to mark the 13 states. There are still the same number of stripes as in 1777; the number of stars, however, has changed as new states joined the union. The flag that was flown on the moon when the American astronauts landed there in 1969 had 50 stars and 13 stripes. It is the same today. Flag Day is June 14, for it was on that day in 1777 that the first American flag was adopted.

Have you gone to any public meetings where the Pledge of Allegiance was said? You will remember that people stood up and placed their right hands over their hearts as they said these words:

PLEDGE OF ALLEGIANCE

I pledge allegiance to the flag of the United States of America and to the Republic for which it stands: One nation under God, indivisible, with liberty and justice for all.

Where did you hear the word *allegiance* before? That's right! In the final step in the naturalization process, before becoming an American citizen, you must take the Oath of Allegiance. Let's read it.

OATH OF ALLEGIANCE

I hereby declare, on oath, that I absolutely and entirely renounce and abjure all allegiance and fidelity to any foreign prince, potentate, state or sovereignty, of whom or which I have heretofore been a subject or citizen; that I will support and defend the Constitution and laws of the United States of America against all enemies, foreign and domestic; that I will bear true faith and allegiance to the same; that I will bear arms on behalf of the United States when required by the law; that I will perform non-combatant service in the Armed Forces of the United States when required by the law; that I will perform work of national importance under civilian direction when required by the law; and that I take this obligation freely without any mental reservation or purpose of evasion, so help me God.

REVIEW

Do you know what these words mean? Write the meanings next to the words. If you are not sure, look up the meaning in the Word List at the end of the book.

1. symbol _____

2. anthem _____

3. "Star-Spangled Banner" _____

4. adopt _____

5. Pledge of Allegiance _____

Now, complete the following sentences in the space provided by adding the word *because* and giving a reason.

Example: We show respect to the flag *because it is the symbol of our country.*

6. The flag is sometimes called the Red, White, and Blue_____

_____

7. The flag has 13 stripes_____

_____

8. It has 50 stars _____

_____

9. Before the American Revolution, most of the colonies used the

British flag _____

10. June 14 is celebrated as Flag Day _____

_____

See the answer key on page 172.

DISPLAYING THE FLAG

Here are two things that we should know about the use of the American flag:

1. When we display the American flag with other flags, our flag should always have the place of honor.

2. The American flag should not be used in advertising (sales, and so on).

Before You Go On to the Final Test:

Review the Steps to Citizenship.
1. Check your eligibility.
2. Send away for the Application for Naturalization and other forms you may need.
3. Become familiar with the requirements for naturalization—both personal and educational.
4. Fill out the forms, file them, and pay the appropriate fees.
5. Practice the answers to important questions.
6. Be able to express yourself in simple English by practicing your reading, writing, and speaking skills.

The Final Test

Test yourself by answering the questions in the space provided. If you get several questions wrong, be sure to review Step 4 again. Even if you do well, be sure to review the reference materials in the Appendix.

1. Who is credited with discovering America? When?_____

_____

2. When was the first permanent settlement in America established? Where?_____

_____

3. Who landed at Plymouth Rock in 1620? _____

_____

4. From what country did we become independent? _____

_____

5. What is taxation without representation? _____

_____

6. When was the Declaration of Independence adopted?_____

_____

7. When was our country first called "The United States of America"? _____

_____

8. Who was the first president of the United States of America?_____

_____

9. Who was Abraham Lincoln?_____

_____

10. What was the Emancipation Proclamation? _____

_____

11. What kind of government does the United States have?_____

_____

12. What is the supreme law of the land? _____

_____

13. When was it adopted? _____

_____

14 . Has it ever been changed? _____

_____

15. What are the branches of the federal government? _____

_____

16. Who makes the laws for the United States?_____

_____

17. What is the highest court in the United States?_____

_____

18. Are there other governments besides the federal government? What are they? _____

_____

19. How many states are there in the United States? _____

_____

20. What are the colors of the American flag? What do they stand for?

_____

21. What is the name of the national anthem?_____

_____

22. Who was president during the Civil War? _____

_____

23. If a law is declared unconstitutional by the Supreme Court, what

happens to it?_____

_____

24. If the president does not approve a bill sent to him by Congress,

what can he do? _____

_____

25. Can the bill still become a law?_____

_____

Check your answers to these questions with the answer key on page 173.

Some Personal Questions

Who is the governor of the state where you live? _____

_____

Who is the mayor, or head, of the local government?_____

_____

Why did you want to come to the United States? _____

_____

Why do you want to become a citizen?_____

_____

Check your answers with a friend.

Step 5—The Naturalization Interview

Some time after you file your N-400, you will be notified to go to be fingerprinted. Some time later, you will be called for the interview. It may take anywhere from six months to two years to be scheduled for the naturalization hearing. You will receive a notice in the mail telling you where and when to go for your interview. (The USCIS is now—May 2004—testing a new program called InfoPass that will allow you to schedule your own interview on the Internet.) It is very important that you keep your appointment. If it is at a location that is unfamiliar to you, take a "practice" trip so that you will know how long it takes to get there. Do not try to change the date! But if you must do so, write a letter to the office where you are supposed to go, asking for a new date and giving the reason for your request. Then you will receive a new appointment. You do not need to bring anyone with you; witnesses are not required. But you do need to bring whatever documents USCIS tells you to bring in the appointment notice. Be early! If you do not show up on time, your case may be closed. Don't let that happen!

The office may be crowded and you may have to wait for your interview. Do not be impatient; keep calm! You have prepared for this test. You have nothing to worry about. Listen carefully to the examiner's questions. During the interview, your ability to understand and to speak English is also being tested. Answer all questions. Follow all instructions. Don't be nervous!

The examiner will have your file and may ask you questions about the N-400, possibly about your residence or your job experience, or why you want to become a citizen. You have reviewed such questions many times. Next will come the test of English and civics. You may be asked to read a passage like those in

Reading Practice in this book. The examiner will also ask you about the United States government and a little history. You know all that!

What you can expect:

For WRITING PRACTICE, some examiners dictate sentences such as:

1. I want to be an American citizen.
2. I have studied the American Constitution.
3. I have a good job.
4. I will do my best to be a worthy citizen.

Get the idea?

For the READING test, you may be asked to read some of the N-400 responses out loud.

For the HISTORY test, or GOVERNMENT, you may be asked to answer about five of the Probability Questions on the following pages, or you may be asked to take a written multiple-choice test that has 20 questions similar to these:

The highest law of the land is

1. The Supreme Court
2. The United Nations
3. The Constitution
4. The Declaration of Independence

Of course, the answer is #3, the Constitution. And so you mark it.

According to the Twenty-Second Amendment to the Constitution, no person can be elected president more than twice. Which of the following presidents was elected more than twice:

1. Theodore Roosevelt
2. Abraham Lincoln
3. George Washington
4. Franklin Roosevelt

The correct answer is Franklin Roosevelt, who was elected to four terms. So, you mark #4. Follow the instructions carefully!

One Applicant's Report

That day finally arrived! The notice had given Anneta the date, time, and place for her citizenship interview. She had marked her calendar, assembled all her papers, and selected her navy blue suit for the occasion. And now that day had arrived. Anneta left the house early enough to arrive 15 minutes before the time scheduled for her interview. To be safe, she had the originals and copies of all her papers, her passport, birth certificate, marriage certificate, and death certificate for her late husband. She had also copies of the income tax forms she had filed. She put them all in a big envelope.

When she arrived, a court officer asked her to raise her right hand and to swear to tell the truth, and nothing but the truth. She did so. That was easy. And the interview began with personal questions such as "What is your address, telephone number, and social security number?" And then some others about her job, her family, whether she had been on public assistance, or had used drugs. She answered them all quickly. One question that she had to look up in her notes was the name of any club or organization she had belonged to in her country of birth. She could easily report the club she had joined since coming to the United States—the Parent-Teachers Association of her daughter's school. The interviewer seemed pleased with her answers. She was then asked questions to determine her knowledge of American history and government.

Some of those questions that she recalled were: What are the colors of the American flag, and what do they represent? What is the capital of the United States? Who is the president? Who was the first president? Who was the president during the Civil War? What is Independence Day, and why do we celebrate it? Who is the governor of New York State, and who is the mayor of New York City? How many states are there? She was also asked to name two states other than New York and New Jersey. Then she had to write a few sentences that the interviewer dictated. She recalled she was asked to write a little about why she wanted to become a citizen. That was easy.

Review of the Probability Questions

These are similar to the 25 questions that we called Probability Questions on page 48, but here they have been rephrased in the way your interviewer may ask them. Do not look back at the ones in Step 2 until you have finished these.

1. How many states are in the United States of America? _____

    _____

2. What are the colors of the flag? _____

3. How many stars are there on our flag? _____

4. What do the stars stand for? _____

5. How many stripes are there? _____

6. What do the stripes stand for? _____

7. What is the Fourth of July? _____

8. Who was the first president of the United States of America?_____

_____

9. Who is president today? _____

10. Who is the vice president? _____

11. What is the Constitution?_____

12. Can the Constitution be changed? If so, what are the changes

called? _____

13. How many branches are in the government?_____

14. What are these branches of our government?_____

15. Which branch makes the laws? _____

16. Which branch carries out the laws? _____

17. Which branch sees to it that all laws are in accordance with the

Constitution? _____

18. What is the highest court in our land? _____

19. What is the Bill of Rights? _____

20. What is the Fourteenth Amendment to the Constitution? _____

_____

21. What are the two houses of Congress?_____

22. Can you name the persons who represent you in Congress? _____

_____

23. Who was Abraham Lincoln?_____

24. What other governments besides the federal government are

there?_____

25. What is the Supreme Court? _____

Now look at the answers under Probability Questions on pages 48–50.

Step 6—
The Last Step—
The Oath

On Monday Anneta received the letter, and on Thursday morning she was on her way to the courthouse in Brooklyn where she would become a citizen of the United States of America. Of course, she was excited, for she would exchange her Green Card for a naturalization certificate. She would belong!

The letter told her to be there at 8 a.m. She arrived early and found herself on line with hundreds of others. When their notices were checked, they were admitted into a large courtroom.

Anneta had hoped for a seat near the front, so she could really hear everything, but that was not to be. Everyone had to be checked by Security for weapons, and then ushered line by line to the seats. Even cell phones were prohibited. Oh well, she wasn't that far back. She smiled at the women next to her, one Asian and the other who seemed to be Russian. She told the women that she was from the Dominican Republic and they smiled back.

Then they waited. At 9 a.m. there were about 200 people seated in the courthouse, when other security guards collected and checked papers. When that was finished, two women judges arrived to take their seats. The audience was quiet and attentive as they came in with three speakers.

Then, the "program" began. Everything was explained. The speakers described the benefits as well as the responsibilities of citizenship. One explained where to go to get a passport; others told about registering to vote. All were very helpful.

At noon, the swearing-in ceremony began. Everyone stood up. Papers were distributed that had the words of the Oath on them. Anneta's eyes were on the huge flag as she read the words.

I hereby declare, on oath, that I absolutely and entirely renounce and abjure all allegiance and fidelity to any foreign prince, potentate, state, or sovereignty, of whom or which I have heretofore been a subject or citizen; that I will support and defend the Constitution and laws of the United States of America against all enemies, foreign and domestic; that I will bear true faith and allegiance to the same; that I will bear arms on behalf of the United States when required by the law; that I will perform non-combatant service in the Armed Forces of the United States when required by the law; that I will perform work of national importance under civilian direction when required by the law; and that I take this obligation freely without any mental reservation or purpose of evasion, so help me God.

One of the speakers read the above, line by line, and asked the audience to repeat each after her. It was a beautiful experience. Hands on heart, they all seemed so serious. Anneta was thrilled to hear the judges.

At the close, there was one more step to take. That was to receive the naturalization certificate from the official at the desk.

Finally, it was over. At 2 p.m. a tired, but happy new citizen, emerged from the Federal building in Brooklyn. She had reached the top step!

NOTE: Many changes from the 5th Edition of this workbook are listed in the For Ready Reference section, under Immigration Update.

In addition, changes, mostly operational, resulting from transition to a new administration, with an emphasis on national security against terrorism, make it seem more difficult today. That is not so. Different names for offices or naturalization procedures do not keep applicants from attaining citizenship, or delay the process.

The chart below will help you understand where you are with respect to the national government, all the way up to the presidency.

U.S. Citizenship and Immigration Services (USCIS) is where it starts. Your first contact is there.

**District Office
USCIS**

which is part of

**U.S. Citizenship and Immigration
Services**

which is part of

**U.S. Department of Homeland
Security**

The Head of This Department Is a Member of the Cabinet of the
President of the United States of America

Figure 20

APPENDIX
★★★★★★★★★★★★★★★★★★★★★★★
For Ready Reference

American English:
Idiomatic Expressions

American English:
Pronunciation Practice

National Holidays

Special Observances

The Declaration of
Independence

The Constitution

Meet the Presidents

Immigration Update

Sample Completed Form
N-400

Word List

Answer Key

American English: Idiomatic Expressions

The American language and customs often are difficult for students. Many teachers find that their pupils encounter unnecessary difficulty with the examination for naturalization. This section provides specific American English language practice and orientation.

For the non-English speaker in the United States, or the newcomer of limited educational background, has difficulty facing differences in language and culture, especially within the context of the naturalization examinations. Everybody has the same problem. Even if you have overcome the basic differences and are on your way to fluency in the new language, you will be helped by the step-by-step presentation in this guide.

For the most part, the naturalization examination is an oral test. The examiner asks the questions; you answer them. Your answer depends on how you interpret the question. If the examiner uses expressions you don't understand, you may be *at a loss!* You can see how important it is to become familiar with different patterns of American speech and with a wide range of special expressions that Americans use as part of their everyday lives. When you practice using these expressions yourself, you will become more confident and successful in your own everyday exchanges with natural-born Americans. Success breeds success! Does that *ring a bell* with you? Of course! *It figures* that this new fluency will help you reach one more step *up the ladder* of success to community participation and, eventually, to real citizenship.

Idioms are groups of words used together in a special sense. They are expressions regularly used in that certain way. There are four examples in what you have just read. The meanings are easy. Say them now—say the entire sentence out loud. Then repeat only the idioms. That's it!

Another example that may help before you study the lists comes from my own experience as a teacher of English.

One day, one of my students raised his hand to ask, "What is a teasy?"

"Do you mean a tease?" I asked.

"Not a tease! A teasy, I hear it all the time. In the subway, many people push and shove. Then some people say, "Take a Teasy!"

I explained the meaning of *take it easy*. And my student was happy.

Take it easy is a common American expression.

Of course, you know that it means to relax, slow down. Another idiom like it is *easy does it*. Say them both now. Make them part of your language!

More Common Idioms

Word	Idiom	Meaning
according	according to	— on the authority
all	all right	— satisfactory
	all at once, all of a sudden	— unexpectedly
	all day (night, week, month)	— continuously
along	go along with	— agree (with an idea)
	get along with	— agree (with a person)
as	as a matter of fact	— really
	as soon as	— when
at	at all (not at all)	— to any degree
be	be over	— finished
bear	bear in mind (keep in mind)	— remember
break	break down	— fall apart
	breakdown	— failure to function
by	by heart	— by memory
	by myself	— alone
	by the way	— incidentally
call	call on	— request help from, visit
	call up	— telephone
catch	catch cold	— get a cold
	catch fire	— get on fire, burn
change	change of $10	— money
	change one's mind	— decide differently
charge	in charge of	— be responsible for
	be charged with (robbery, murder, etc.)	— having a statement made against
count	count on	— depend
cover	to cover up	— to hide something,
	cover up	something concealed
cross	to cross the street	— to go across
	to cross out	— to draw a line through
day	day off	— nonworking day
	day in, day out	— all the time

Word	Idiom	Meaning
do	to do one's best	— to try hard
	what do you *do*?	— what is your work?
		(answer: *I'm a* lawyer, plumber, etc.)
	do over	— to correct
else	what else, where else	— besides the answer given
entitled	to be entitled to	— to deserve (by law)
every	every now and then	— from time to time
	every other day	— on two days with a day in between
figure out	can you figure out the meaning?	— estimate, determine
file	to file a claim, a report, document	— to turn over a paper to the proper authority
fill	fill in (the form, etc.), fill out	— to put in what is necessary
find	to find out	— to learn
for	for the present, for the time being	— temporarily
fringe	fringe benefits	— special good things that go with some jobs
get	to get along	— to succeed
	to get along with	— to be friends with
	to get away with	— to escape
	to get in touch with	— to communicate with
going	going to (in the future)	— will go, will do something
had	had better	— it would be a good idea to
hand	hand in	— to submit a paper
	on hand	— in stock
hang	to hang up	— to put back
hear	to hear from	— to get word from
hold	to hold on	— to wait
	to hold off	— to delay
in	in a hurry	— in a rush
	in the long run	— over a long period of time
	in time	— soon enough
just	just a minute	— soon
	just so	— correct
keep	to keep an eye on	— to watch
	to keep in touch with	— to continue communication
	to keep up	— to continue
know	to know by heart	— to memorize
lay	to lay off	— to get let go from a job
little	little by little	— gradually
look	to look after	— to care for
	to look forward to	— to anticipate
	to look into	— to check
	to look up	— to search for

American English: Idiomatic Expressions

Word	Idiom	Meaning
make	to make an appointment	— to set a date for
	to make clear	— to explain
meet	to meet the requirements	— to be eligible
mixed	mixed up	— confused
more	more or less	— for the most part
never	never mind	— forget it
nothing	nothing wrong, nothing the matter	— everything is okay
now	now and then	— once in a while
on	on the radio, television, etc.	— in a program
	on time	— punctual
out	out of order	— not functioning
	out of the question	— not possible
over	do it over and over	— to repeat something many times
pass	pass judgment on	— give an opinion on
	pass a law	— enact a bill
	to pass away	— to die
pick	pick out	— choose
	to pick up	— to take
play	to play ball	— to go along with
point	to point out	— to call attention to
put	to put down	— to suppress
	to put on	— to assume
	to put off	— to postpone
quiet	quiet down	— stop making noise or speaking
quite	quite a few	— many
rather	rather than	— instead of
responsible	responsible for	— in charge of
right	right away	— very soon
say	say the word	— give the order
	to say nothing of	— not to mention
scam	to pull a scam	— trick to deceive
see	to see about	— to check into
	to see to it	— to ensure
take	take an oath	— swear
	take one's time	— go slowly
think	think it over	— consider it carefully
time	to have time	— plenty of time left
up	up-to-date	— timely
used	used to	— in the past

Word	Idiom	Meaning
vain	in vain	— without success
very	the very thing	— exactly right
walk	to walk out	— to leave
while	a little while	— a short time
without	to do without	— to lack
work	to work out	— to exercise
write	to write away for	— to send for

As you can see, English is an idiomatic language. These are only a sample of those you may hear in everyday speech.

REVIEW

As a review, see if you can fill in the blanks in the following sentences with an idiomatic expression from the list.

1. I_____live in Chicago, but now I live in New York.

2. I_____to pay my taxes; they are not due until April.

3. It is_____for me to lend my friend money at this time.

4. Business is so bad, the company will have to_____some workers.

5. Joe worked in a dress factory for_____last year.

6. Please_____for an application for me!

7. Olga is_____to bringing her husband into this country soon.

8. She_____him last week that his application was being checked.

9. "_____, it takes time," said Olga's teacher.

10. "He will have a nervous_____ if he doesn't get his papers soon," she answered.

Check your answer to these questions with the answer key on page 173.

American English: Pronunciation Practice

Even after many years in their new country, some immigrants still experience difficulties with the *consonant sounds* of American English. If you have problems with Ls, Rs, Bs, Hs, Vs, Th blends, and others, this section is for you.

Practice, practice the positions of the mouth, lips, and tongue, in order to produce the sound correctly. Exaggerate the directions. Use a mirror. In any case, do it every day!

	Say	*Repeat*
Beginning L and R Sounds		
Put tip of tongue behind upper teeth.	let	Let Lulu do it.
	light	Light the lamp.
	right	The answer is right.
	run	Run the race.
T and D, N and S		
Put tip of tongue above upper front teeth.	tell	Tell me the time.
	tight	Too tight.
	don't	Don't run!
	did	Did Dot do her lesson?
	dull	It was too dull.
	no, not	Not at all!
	sunset	The sun sets late in Sweden.

113

TH
Open lips a little; put
tongue between teeth.

the
this
think

This is the time
to think about supper.

CH, SH, Y, J, and Z
Put middle of tongue
against top of mouth.

chin
ship
join

measure

Place your chin on the ship
   in the bottle.
Charles and John joined the
   union yesterday.
Measure the chair to see if it is
   larger than the old chair.

H Sound
Part your lips and blow.

he
her
home

He asked her to show him
   her new home.

M, P, B, and W (WH) Sounds
Bring your lips together.

Mama
move
Papa
baby
will
what, where

The baby's first word
   was *Papa,* not *Mama.*
What will you do?
Where will you go?

F and V
Bite your lower lip.

fat
very

The very fat man wants
   to be thin.

K, X, G, and NG
Put back of tongue against
top of mouth.

key
exit
girl
sing a song

Keep the exit door locked
   with a key.
The girl keeps singing a
   song all day long.

This is a simple approach to some sounds that may be difficult for you. Practice them as often as you can. You will be glad when it is time for your naturalization examination!

National Holidays

You may be asked why we celebrate the national holiday nearest to the time of your naturalization examination. You may wonder why businesses have special sales on February 22. Of course, you know that the Fourth of July/Independence Day is our most important national holiday. Do you know why the following holidays are celebrated nationally?

January 1	New Year's Day
January 15	Birthday of Martin Luther King, Jr.
February 22	Birthday of George Washington
May 30	Memorial Day
July 4	The Fourth of July/Independence Day
First Monday in September	Labor Day
October 12	Columbus Day
November 11	Veterans Day
Fourth Thursday in November	Thanksgiving Day
December 25	Christmas

Some of the days are changed to Monday or Friday, to give people a three-day weekend. And, if the holiday falls on a Sunday, the next day also is celebrated as a holiday.

Special Observances

These are not holidays, but special observances that are held in different parts of the United States.

February 12	Lincoln's Birthday
February 14	St. Valentine's Day
March 17	St. Patrick's Day
Second Sunday in May	Mother's Day
June 14	Flag Day
Third Sunday in June	Father's Day
September 17	Citizenship Day
October 24	United Nations Day
First Tuesday	Election Day
after first Monday in November	

Religious holy dates, of course, also are widely observed.

REVIEW: Holidays and Observances

Read the dates in Column I aloud. Then read Column II. Match the letters with the numbers by drawing lines from one to the other. Lastly, put the letters in the space next to the numbered items. Do it like this:

1. Fourth Thursday ___c___ ———— **c.** Thanksgiving Day
   in November

COLUMN I		COLUMN II
1. October 12	_____	**a.** St. Patrick's Day
2. December 25	_____	**b.** Labor Day
3. March 17	_____	**c.** Martin Luther King Jr.'s Birthday
4. January 15	_____	**d.** Veterans Day
5. First Monday in September	_____	**e.** Columbus Day
6. February 22	_____	**f.** Lincoln's Birthday
7. June 14	_____	**g.** Memorial Day
8. July 4	_____	**h.** Flag Day
9. February 12	_____	**i.** George Washington's Birthday
10. May 30	_____	**j.** Christmas Day
		k. Independence Day

Turn the book upside down to find the right answers.

The Declaration of Independence

In Congress, July 4, 1776

The Unanimous Declaration of the Thirteen United States of America

When in the course of human events, it becomes necessary for one people to dissolve the political bands which have connected them with another, and to assume among the powers of the earth, the separate and equal station to which the laws of Nature and of Nature's God entitle them, a decent respect to the opinions of mankind requires that they should declare the causes which impel them to the separation.

We hold these truths to be self-evident, that all men are created equal, that they are endowed by their Creator with certain unalienable rights, that among these are life, liberty and the pursuit of happiness. That to secure these rights, governments are instituted among men, deriving their just powers from the consent of the governed,— That whenever any form of government becomes destructive of these ends, it is the right of the people to alter or to abolish it, and to institute new government, laying its foundation on such principles and organizing its powers in such form, as to them shall seem most likely to effect their safety and happiness. Prudence, indeed, will dictate that governments long established should not be changed for light and transient causes; and accordingly all experience hath shown, that mankind are more disposed to suffer, while evils are sufferable, than to right themselves by abolishing the forms to which they are accustomed. But when a long train of abuses and usurpations, pursuing invariably the same object evinces a design to reduce them under absolute despotism, it is their right, it is their duty, to throw off such government, and to provide new guards for their future security.—Such has been the patient sufferance of these colonies; and such is now the necessity which constrains them to alter their former systems of government. The history of the present King of Great Britain is a history of repeated injuries and usurpations, all having in direct object the establishment of an absolute tyranny over these states. To prove this, let facts be submitted to a candid world.

He has refused his assent to laws, the most wholesome and necessary for the public good.

He has forbidden his governors to pass laws of immediate and pressing importance, unless suspended in their operation till his assent should be obtained; and when so suspended, he has utterly neglected to attend to them.

He has refused to pass other laws for the accommodation of large districts of people, unless those people would relinquish the right of representation in the legislature, a right inestimable to them and formidable to tyrants only.

He has called together legislative bodies at places unusual, uncomfortable, and distant from the depository of their public records, for the sole purpose of fatiguing them into compliance with his measures.

He has dissolved Representative Houses repeatedly, for opposing with manly firmness his invasion on the rights of the people.

He has refused for a long time, after such dissolutions, to cause others to be elected; whereby the legislative powers, incapable of annihilation, have returned to the people at large for their exercise; the state remaining in the meantime exposed to all the dangers of invasion from without, and convulsions within.

He has endeavoured to prevent the population of these states; for that purpose obstructing the laws for naturalization of foreigners; refusing to pass others to encourage their migrations hither, and raising the conditions of new appropriations of lands.

He has obstructed the administration of justice, by refusing his assent to laws for establishing judiciary powers.

He has made judges dependent on his will alone, for the tenure of their offices, and the amount and payment of their salaries.

He has erected a multitude of new offices, and sent hither swarms of officers to harass our people, and eat out their substance.

He has kept among us, in times of peace, standing armies without the consent of our legislatures.

He has affected to render the military independent of and superior to the civil power.

He has combined with others to subject us to a jurisdiction foreign to our constitution, and unacknowledged by our laws; giving his assent to their acts of pretended legislation:

For quartering large bodies of armed troops among us:

For protecting them, by a mock trial, from punishment for any murders which they should commit on the inhabitants of these states:

For cutting off our trade with all parts of the world:

For imposing taxes on us without our consent:

For depriving us in many cases, of the benefits of trial by jury:

For transporting us beyond seas to be tried for pretended offenses:

For abolishing the free system of English laws in a neighbouring province, establishing therein an arbitrary government, and enlarging its boundaries so as to render it at once an example and fit instrument for introducing the same absolute rule into these colonies:

For taking away our charters, abolishing our most valuable laws, and altering fundamentally the forms of our government.

For suspending our own legislatures, and declaring themselves invested with power to legislate for us in all cases whatsoever. He has abdicated government here, by declaring us out of his protection and waging war against us.

He has plundered our seas, ravaged our coasts, burnt our towns, and destroyed the lives of our people.

He is at this time transporting large armies of foreign mercenaries to complete the works of death, desolation and tyranny, already begun with circumstances of cruelty and perfidy scarcely paralleled in the most barbarous ages and totally unworthy the head of a civilized nation.

He has constrained our fellow citizens taken captive on the high seas to bear arms against their country, to become the executioners of their friends and brethren, or to fall themselves by their hands.

He has excited domestic insurrections amongst us, and has endeavoured to bring on the inhabitants of our frontiers, the merciless Indian savages, whose known rule of warfare is an undistinguished destruction of all ages, sexes, and conditions.

In every stage of these oppressions we have petitioned for redress in the most humble terms: Our repeated petitions have been answered only by repeated injury. A prince, whose character is thus marked by every act which may define a tyrant, is unfit to be the ruler of a free people.

Nor have we been wanting in attentions to our British brethren. We have warned them from time to time of attempts by their legislature to extend an unwarrantable jurisdiction over us. We have reminded them of the circumstances of our emigration and settlement here. We have appealed to their native justice and magnanimity, and we have conjured them by the ties of our common kindred to disavow these usurpations, which, would inevitably interrupt our connections and correspondence. They too have been deaf to the voice of justice and of consanguinity. We must, therefore, acquiesce in the necessary which denounces our separation, and hold them, as we hold the rest of mankind, enemies in war, in peace friends.

WE, THEREFORE the Representatives of the United States of America, in General Congress, Assembled, appealing to the Supreme Judge of the world for the rectitude of our intentions, do, in the name, and by authority of the good people of these colonies, solemnly publish and declare, That these United Colonies are, and of right ought to be FREE AND INDEPENDENT STATES; that they are absolved from all allegiance to the British Crown, and that all political connection between them and the state of Great Britain, is and ought to be totally dissolved; and that as free and independent states, they have full power to levy war, conclude peace, contract alliances, establish commerce, and to do all other acts and things which independent states may of right do. And for the support of this Declaration, with a firm reliance on the protection of Divine Providence, we mutually pledge to each other our lives, our fortunes, and our sacred honor.

JOHN HANCOCK.

New Hampshire

JOSIAH BARTLETT   MATTHEW THORNTON
WM. WHIPPLE

Massachusetts Bay

SAML ADAMS   ROBT TREAT PAINE
JOHN ADAMS   ELBRIDGE GERRY

Rhode Island

STEP. HOPKINS   WILLIAM ELLERY

Connecticut

ROGER SHERMAN   WM. WILLIAMS
SAML HUNTINGTON   OLIVER WOLCOTT

New York

WM. FLOYD   FRANS. LEWIS
PHIL. LIVINGSTON   LEWIS MORRIS

New Jersey

RICHD. STOCKTON   JOHN HART
JNO WITHERSPOON   ABRA CLARK .
FRAS. HOPKINSON

Pennsylvania

ROBT MORRIS   JAS. SMITH
BENJAMIN RUSH   GEO. TAYLOR
BENJA. FRANKLIN   JAMES WILSON
JOHN MORTON   GEO. ROSS
GEO. CLYMER

Delaware

CAESAR RODNEY   THO M'KEAN
GEO READ

Maryland

SAMUEL CHASE   CHARLES CARROLL
WM. PACA   of Carrollton

Virginia

GEORGE WYTHE   THOS. NELSON JR.
RICHARD HENRY LEE   FRANCIS LIGHTFOOT LEE
TH JEFFERSON   CARTER BRAXTON
BENJA. HARRISON

North Carolina

WM HOOPER   JOHN PENN
JOSEPH HEWES

South Carolina

EDWARD RUTLEDGE   THOS HEYWARD JUNR.
THOMAS LYNCH JUNR.   ARTHUR MIDDLETON

Georgia

BUTTON GWINNETT   GEO WALTON
LYMAN HALL

The Constitution

Preamble

WE THE PEOPLE of the United States, in order to form a more perfect Union, establish justice, insure domestic tranquility, provide for the common defense, promote the general welfare, and secure the blessings of liberty to ourselves and our posterity, do ordain and establish this Constitution for the United States of America.

Article I

Section 1. All legislative powers herein granted shall be vested in a Congress of the United States, which shall consist of a Senate and House of Representatives.

Section 2. The House of Representatives shall be composed of members chosen every second year by the people of the several states, and the electors in each state shall have the qualifications requisite for electors of the most numerous branch of the state legislature.

No person shall be a Representative who shall not have attained to the age of twenty-five years, and been seven years a citizen of the United States, and who shall not, when elected, be an inhabitant of that state in which he shall be chosen.

Representatives and direct taxes shall be apportioned among the several states which may be included within this Union, according to their respective numbers, which shall be determined by adding to the whole number of free persons, including those bound to service for a term of years, and excluding Indians not taxed, three-fifths of all other persons. The actual enumeration shall be made within three years after the first meeting of the Congress of the United States, and within every subsequent term of ten years, in such manner as they shall by law direct. The number of Representatives shall not exceed one for every thirty thousand, but each state shall have at least one representative; and until such enumeration shall be made, the state of New Hampshire shall be entitled to choose three,

Massachusetts eight, Rhode Island and Providence Plantations one, Connecticut five, New York six, New Jersey four, Pennsylvania eight, Delaware one, Maryland six, Virginia ten, North Carolina five, South Carolina five, and Georgia three.

When vacancies happen in the representation from any state, the executive authority thereof shall issue writs of election to fill such vacancies.

The House of Representatives shall choose their Speaker and other officers; and shall have the sole power of impeachment.

Section 3. The Senate of the United States shall be composed of two Senators from each state, chosen by the legislature thereof, for six years and each Senator shall have one vote.

Immediately after they shall be assembled in consequence of the first election, they shall be divided as equally as may be into three classes. The seats of the Senators of the first class shall be vacated at the expiration of the second year, of the second class at the expiration of the fourth year, and of the third class at the expiration of the sixth year so that one-third may be chosen every second year; and if vacancies happen by resignation, or otherwise, during the recess of the legislature of any state, the executive thereof may make temporary appointments until the next meeting of the legislature, which shall then fill such vacancies.

No person shall be a Senator who shall not have attained to the age of thirty years, and been nine years a citizen of the United States, and who shall not, when elected, be an inhabitant of that state for which he shall be chosen.

The Vice President of the United States shall be President of the Senate, but shall have no vote, unless they be equally divided.

The Senate shall choose their other officers, and also a President pro tempore, in the absence of the Vice President, or when he shall exercise the office of President of the United States.

The Senate shall have the sole power to try all impeachments. When sitting for that purpose, they shall be on oath or affirmation. When the President of the United States is tried, the Chief Justice shall preside: And no person shall be convicted without the concurrence of two-thirds of the members present.

Judgment in cases of impeachment shall not extend further than to removal from office, and disqualification to hold and enjoy any office of honor, trust or profit under the United States: but the party convicted shall nevertheless be liable and subject to indictment, trial, judgment and punishment, according to law.

Section 4. The times, places and manner of holding elections for Senators and Representatives, shall be prescribed in each state by the legislature thereof; but the Congress may at any time by law make or alter such regulations, except as to the place of choosing Senators.

The Congress shall assemble at least once in every year, and such meeting shall be on the first Monday in December, unless they shall by law appoint a different day.

Section 5. Each House shall be the judge of the elections, returns and qualifications of its own members, and a majority of each shall constitute a quorum to do business; but a smaller number may adjourn from day to day, and may be authorized to compel the attendance of absent members, in such manner, and under such penalties as each House may provide.

Each House may determine the rules of its proceedings, punish its members for disorderly behaviour, and, with the concurrence of two-thirds, expel a member.

Each House shall keep a journal of its proceedings, and from time to time publish the same, excepting such parts as may in their judgment require secrecy; and the yeas and nays of the members of either House on any question shall, at the desire of one-fifth of those present, be entered on the journal.

Neither House, during the session of Congress, shall, without the consent of the other, adjourn for more than three days, not to any other place than that in which the two Houses shall be sitting.

Section 6. The Senators and Representatives shall receive a compensation for their services, to be ascertained by law, and paid out of the Treasury of the United States. They shall in all cases, except treason, felony and breach of the peace, be privileged from arrest during their attendance at the session of their respective Houses, and in going to and returning from the same; and for any speech or debate in either House, they shall not be questioned in any other place.

No Senator or Representative shall, during the time for which he was elected, be appointed to any civil office under the authority of the United States, which shall have been created, or the emoluments whereof shall have been increased during such time; and no person holding any office under the United States, shall be a member of either House during his continuance in office.

Section 7. All bills for raising revenue shall originate in the House of Representatives; but the Senate may propose or concur with amendments as on other bills.

Every bill which shall have passed the House of Representatives and the Senate, shall, before it becomes a law, be presented to the President of the United States; if he approves he shall sign it, but if not he shall return it, with his objections to that House in which it shall have originated, who shall enter the objections at large on their journal, and proceed to reconsider it. If after such reconsideration two thirds of that House shall agree to pass the bill, it shall be sent, together with the objections, to the other House, by which it shall likewise be reconsidered, and if approved by two thirds of that House, it shall become a law. But in all such cases the votes of both Houses shall be determined by yeas and nays, and the names of the persons voting for and against the bill shall be entered on the journal of each House respectively. If any bill shall not be returned by the President within ten days (Sundays excepted) after it shall have been presented to him, the same shall be a law, in like manner as if he had signed it, unless the Congress by their adjournment prevent its return, in which case it shall not be a law.

Every order, resolution, or vote to which the concurrence of the Senate and House of Representatives may be necessary (except on a question of adjournment) shall be presented to the President of the United States; and before the same shall take effect, shall be approved by him, or being disapproved by him, shall be repassed by two thirds of the Senate and House of Representatives, according to the rules and limitations prescribed in the case of a bill.

Section 8. The Congress shall have power to lay and collect taxes, duties, imposts and excises, to pay the debts and provide for the common defense and general welfare of the United States; but all duties, imposts and excises shall be uniform throughout the United States;

To borrow money on the credit of the United States;

To regulate commerce with foreign nations, and among the several States, and with the Indian tribes;

To establish a uniform rule of naturalization, and uniform laws on the subject of bankruptcies throughout the United States;

To coin money, regulate the value thereof, and of foreign coin, and fix the standard of weights and measures;

To provide for the punishment of counterfeiting the securities and current coin of the United States;

To establish post offices and post roads;

To promote the progress of science and useful arts, by securing for limited times to authors and inventors the exclusive right to their respective writings and discoveries;

To constitute tribunals inferior to the Supreme Court;

To define and punish piracies and felonies committed on the high seas, and offenses against the law of nations;

To declare war, grant letters of marque and reprisal, and make rules concerning captures on land and water;

To raise and support armies, but no appropriation of money to that use shall be for a longer term than two years;

To provide and maintain a Navy;

To make rules for the government and regulation of the land and naval forces;

To provide for calling forth the militia to execute the laws of the Union, suppress insurrections and repel invasions;

To provide for organizing, arming, and disciplining the militia, and for governing such part of them as may be employed in the service of the United States, reserving to the states respectively, the appointment of the officers, and the authority of training the militia according to the discipline prescribed by Congress;

To exercise exclusive legislation in all cases whatsoever, over such District (not exceeding ten miles square) as may, by cession of particular states, and the acceptance of Congress, become the seat of the government of the United States, and to exercise like authority over all places purchased by the consent of the legislature of the state in which the same shall be, for the erection of forts, magazines, arsenals, dock-yards, and other needful buildings;—and

To make all laws which shall be necessary and proper for carrying into execution the foregoing powers, and all other powers vested by this Constitution in the government of the United States, or in any department or officer thereof.

Section 9. The migration or importation of such persons as any of the states now existing shall think proper to admit, shall not be prohibited by the Congress prior to the year one thousand eight hundred and eight, but a tax or duty may be imposed on such importation, not exceeding ten dollars for each person.

The privilege of the writ of habeas corpus shall not be suspended, unless when in cases of rebellion or invasion the public safety may require it.

No bill of attainder or ex post facto law shall be passed.

No capitation, or other direct, tax shall be laid, unless in proportion to the census or enumeration herein before directed to be taken.

No tax or duty shall be laid on articles exported from any state.

No preference shall be given by any regulation of commerce or revenue to the ports of one state over those of another: nor shall vessels bound to, or from, one state, be obliged to enter, clear, or pay duties in another.

No money shall be drawn from the Treasury, but in consequence of appropriations made by law; and a regular statement and account of the receipts and expenditures of all public money shall be published from time to time.

No title of nobility shall be granted by the United States: And no person holding any office of profit or trust under them, shall, without the consent of the Congress, accept of any present, emolument, office, or title, of any kind whatever, from any King, Prince, or foreign state.

Section 10. No state shall enter into any treaty, alliance, or confederation; grant letters of marque and reprisal; coin money; emit bills of credit; make any thing but gold and silver coin a tender in payment of debts; pass any bill of attainder, ex post facto law, or law impairing the obligation of contracts, or grant any title of nobility.

No state shall, without the consent of the Congress, lay any imposts or duties on imports or exports, except what may be absolutely necessary for executing its inspection laws: and the net produce of all duties and imposts, laid by any state on imports or exports, shall be for the use of the Treasury of the United States; and all such laws shall be subject to the revision and control of the Congress.

No state shall, without the consent of Congress, lay any duty of tonnage, keep troops, or ships of war in time of peace, enter into any agreement or compact with another state, or with a foreign power, or engage in war, unless actually invaded, or in such imminent danger as will not admit of delay.

Article II

Section 1. The executive power shall be vested in a President of the United States of America. He shall hold his office during the term of four years, and, together with the Vice President, chosen for the same term, be elected, as follows:

Each state, shall appoint, in such manner as the legislature thereof may direct, a number of electors, equal to the whole number of Senators and Representatives to which the state may be entitled in the Congress; but no Senator or Representative, or person holding an office of trust or profit under the United States, shall be appointed an elector.

The electors shall meet in their respective states, and vote by ballot for two persons, of whom one at least shall not be an inhabitant of the same state with themselves. And they shall make a list of all the persons voted for, and of the number of votes for each; which list they shall sign and certify, and transmit sealed to the seat of the government of the United States, directed to the President of the Senate. The President of the Senate shall, in the presence of the Senate and House of Representatives, open all the certificates, and the votes shall then be counted. The person having the greatest number of votes shall be the President, if such number be a majority of the whole number of electors appointed; and if there be more than one who have such majority, and have an equal number of votes, then the House of Representatives shall immediately choose by ballot one of them for President; and if no person have a majority, then from the five highest on the list the said House shall in like manner choose the President. But in choosing the President, the votes shall be taken by states, the representation from each state having one vote; a quorum for this purpose shall consist of a member or members from two thirds of the states, and a majority of all the states shall be necessary to a choice.

In every case, after the choice of the President, the person having the greatest number of votes of the electors shall be the Vice President. But if there should remain two or more who have equal votes, the Senate shall choose from them by ballot the Vice President.

The Congress may determine the time of choosing the electors, and the day on which they shall give their votes; which day shall be the same throughout the United States.

No person except a natural born citizen, or a citizen of the United States, at the time of the adoption of this Constitution, shall be eligible to the office of President; neither shall any person be eligible to that office who shall not have attained to the age of thirty-five years, and been fourteen years a resident within the United States.

In case of the removal of the President from office, or of his death, resignation, or inability to discharge the powers and duties of the said office, the same shall devolve on the Vice President, and the Congress may by law provide for the case of removal, death, resignation, or inability, both of the President and Vice President, declaring what officer shall then act as President, and such officer shall act accordingly, until the disability be removed, or a President shall be elected. The President shall, at stated times, receive for his services, a compensation, which shall neither be increased nor diminished during the period for which he shall have been elected, and he shall not receive within that period any other emolument from the United States, or any of them.

Before he enters on the execution of his office, he shall take the following oath or affirmation:— "I do solemnly swear (or affirm) that I will faithfully execute the office of President of the United States, and will to the best of my ability, preserve, protect and defend the Constitution of the United States."

Section 2. The President shall be commander in chief of the Army and Navy of the United States, and of the militia of the several States, when called into the actual service of the United States; he may require the opinion, in writing, of the principal officer in each of the executive departments, upon any subject relating to the duties of their respective offices, and he shall have power to grant reprieves and pardons for offenses against the United States, except in cases of impeachment.

He shall have power, by and with the advice and consent of the Senate, to make treaties, provided two thirds of the Senators present concur; and he shall nominate, and by and with the advice and consent of the Senate, shall appoint ambassadors, other public ministers and consuls, judges of the Supreme Court, and all other officers of the United States, whose appointments are not herein otherwise provided for, and which shall be established by law: but the Congress may by law vest the appointment of such inferior officers, as they think proper, in the President alone, in the courts of law, or in the heads of departments.

The President shall have power to fill up all vacancies that may happen during the recess of the Senate, by granting commissions which shall expire at the end of their next session.

Section 3. He shall from time to time give to the Congress information of the state of the Union, and recommend to their consideration such measures as he shall judge necessary and expedient; he may, on extraordinary occasions, convene both Houses, or either of them, and in case of disagreement between them, with respect to the time of adjournment, he may adjourn them to such time as he shall think proper; he shall receive ambassadors and other public ministers; he shall take care that the laws be faithfully executed, and shall commission all the officers of the United States.

Section 4. The President, Vice President and all civil officers of the United States, shall be removed from office on impeachment for, and conviction of, treason, bribery, or other high crimes and misdemeanors.

Article III

Section 1. The judicial power of the United States, shall be vested in one Supreme Court, and in such inferior courts as the Congress may from time to time ordain and establish. The judges, both of the supreme and inferior courts, shall hold their offices during good behaviour, and shall, at stated times, receive for their services, a compensation which shall not be diminished during their continuance in office.

Section 2. The judicial power shall extend to all cases, in law and equity, arising under this Constitution, the laws of the United States, and treaties made, or which shall be made, under their authority;—to all cases affecting ambassadors, other public ministers and consuls;—to all cases of admiralty and maritime jurisdiction;—to controversies to which the United States shall be a party;—to controversies between two or more states;—between a state and citizens of another state;—between citizens of different states;—between citizens of the same state claiming lands under grants of different states, and between a state, or the citizens thereof, and foreign states, citizens or subjects.

In all cases affecting ambassadors, other public ministers and consuls, and those in which a state shall be a party, the Supreme Court shall have original jurisdiction. In all the other cases before mentioned, the Supreme Court shall have appellate jurisdiction, both as to law and fact, with such exceptions, and under such regulations as the Congress shall make.

The trial of all crimes, except in cases of impeachment, shall be by jury; and such trial shall be held in the state where the said crimes shall have been committed; but when not committed within any state, the trial shall be at such place or places as the Congress may by law have directed.

Section 3. Treason against the United States, shall consist only in levying war against them, or in adhering to their enemies, giving them aid and comfort. No person shall be convicted of treason unless on the testimony of two witnesses to the same overt act, or on confession in open court.

The Congress shall have power to declare the punishment of treason, but no attainder of treason shall work corruption of blood, or forfeiture except during the life of the person attained.

Article IV

Section 1. Full faith and credit shall be given in each state to the public acts, records, and judicial proceedings of every other state. And the Congress may by general laws prescribe the manner in which such acts, records and proceedings shall be proved, and the effect thereof.

Section 2. The citizens of each state shall be entitled to all privileges and immunities of citizens in the several states.

A person charged in any state with treason, felony, or other crime, who shall flee from justice, and be found in another state, shall on demand of the executive authority of the state from which he fled, be delivered up, to be removed to the state having jurisdiction of the crime.

No person held to service or labour in one state, under the laws thereof, escaping into another, shall, in consequence of any law or regulation therein, be discharged from such service or labour, but shall be delivered up on claim of the party to whom such service or labour may be due.

Section 3. New states may be admitted by the Congress into this Union; but no new state shall be formed or erected within the jurisdiction of any other state; nor any state be formed by the junction of two or more states, or parts of states, without the consent of the legislature of the states concerned as well as of the Congress.

The Congress shall have power to dispose of and make all needful rules and regulations respecting the territory or other property belonging to the United States; and nothing in this Constitution shall be so construed as to prejudice any claims of the United States, or of any particular state.

Section 4. The United States shall guarantee to every state in this Union a republican form of government, and shall protect each of them against invasion; and on application of the legislature, or of the executive (when the legislature cannot be convened) against domestic violence.

Article V

The Congress, whenever two thirds of both Houses shall deem it necessary, shall propose amendments to this Constitution, or on the application of the legislatures of two thirds of the several states, shall call a convention for proposing amendments, which, in either case, shall be valid to all intents and purposes, as part of this Constitution, when ratified by the legislatures of three fourths of the several States, or by conventions in three fourths thereof, as the one or the other mode of ratification may be proposed by the Congress; provided that no amendment which may be made prior to the year one thousand eight hundred and eight shall in any manner affect the first and fourth clauses in the Ninth Section of the First Article; and that no state, without its consent, shall be deprived of its equal suffrage in the Senate.

Article VI

All debts contracted and engagements entered into, before the adoption of this Constitution, shall be as valid against the United States under this Constitution, as under the Confederation.

This Constitution, and the laws of the United States which shall be made in pursuance thereof; and all treaties made, or which shall be made, under the authority of the United States, shall be the supreme law of the land; and the judges in every state shall be bound thereby, any thing in the Constitution or laws of any State to the contrary notwithstanding.

The Senators and Representatives before mentioned, and the members of the several state legislatures, and all executive and judicial officers, both of the United States and of the several states, shall be bound by oath or affirmation, to support this Constitution; but no religious test shall ever be required as a qualification to any office or public trust under the United States.

Article VII

The ratification of the conventions of nine states shall be sufficient for the establishment of this Constitution between the states so ratifying the same.

Done in convention by the unanimous consent of the states present the seventeenth day of September in the year of our Lord one thousand seven hundred and eighty seven and of the independence of the United States of America the twelfth. In witness whereof we have hereunto subscribed out names,

Go. WASHINGTON—*Presid't,*
and deputy from Virginia
Attest WILLIAM JACKSON *Secretary*

New Hampshire
JOHN LANGDON   NICHOLAS GILMAN

Massachusetts
NATHANIEL GORHAM   RUFUS KING

Connecticut
WM. SAML. JOHNSON   ROGER SHERMAN

New York
ALEXANDER HAMILTON

New Jersey
WIL. LIVINGSTON   WM. PATERSON
DAVID BREARLEY   JONA. DAYTON

Pennsylvania
B. FRANKLIN   THOS. FITZSIMONS
THOMAS MIFFLIN   JARED INGERSOLL
ROBT MORRIS   JAMES WILSON
GEO. CLYMER   GOUV MORRIS

Delaware
GEO. READ   RICHARD BASSETT
GUNNING BEDFORD JUN   JACO. BROOM
JOHN DICKINSON

Maryland
JAMES MCHENRY   DANL CARROLL
DAN OF ST THOS.
  JENIFER

Virginia
JOHN BLAIR—   JAMES MADISON JR.

North Carolina
WM. BLOUNT   HU WILLIAMSON
RICHD. DOBBS SPAIGHT

South Carolina
J. RUTLEDGE   CHARLES PICKNEY
CHARLES COTESWORTH   PIERCE BUTLER
  PICKNEY

Georgia
WILLIAM FEW   ABR BALDWIN

Amendments

Article I

Congress shall make no law respecting an establishment of religion, or prohibiting the free exercise thereof; or abridging the freedom of speech, or of the press; or the right of the people peaceably to assemble, and to petition the government for a redress of grievances.

Article II

A well-regulated militia, being necessary to the security of a free state, the right of the people to keep and bear arms, shall not be infringed.

Article III

No soldier shall, in time of peace be quartered in any house, without the consent of the owner, nor in time of war, but in a manner to be prescribed by law.

Article IV

The right of the people to be secure in their persons, houses, papers, and effects, against unreasonable searches and seizures, shall not be violated, and no warrants shall issue, but upon probable cause, supported by oath or affirmation, and particularly describing the place to be searched, and the persons or things to be seized.

Article V

No person shall be held to answer for a capital, or otherwise infamous crime, unless on a presentment or indictment of a Grand Jury, except in cases arising in the land or naval forces, or in the militia, when in actual service in time of war or public danger; nor shall any person be subject for the same offense to be twice put in jeopardy of life or limb; nor shall be compelled in any criminal case to be a witness against himself, nor be deprived of life, liberty, or property, without due process of law; nor shall private property be taken for public use, without just compensation.

Article VI

In all criminal prosecutions, the accused shall enjoy the right to a speedy and public trial, by an impartial jury of the state and district wherein the crime shall have been committed, which district shall have been previously ascertained by law, and to be informed of the nature and cause of the accusation; to be confronted with the witnesses against him; to have compulsory process for obtaining witnesses in his favor, and to have the assistance of counsel for his defense.

Article VII

In suits at common law, where the value in controversy shall exceed twenty dollars, the right of trial by jury shall be preserved, and no fact tried by a jury, shall be otherwise reexamined in any court of the United States, than according to the rules of the common law.

Article VIII

Excessive bail shall not be required, nor excessive fines imposed, nor cruel and unusual punishments inflicted.

Article IX

The enumeration in the Constitution, of certain rights, shall not be construed to deny or disparage others retained by the people.

Article X

The powers not delegated to the United States by the Constitution, nor prohibited by it to the states, are reserved to the states respectively, or to the people.

Article XI

The judicial power of the United States shall not be construed to extend to any suit in law or equity, commenced or prosecuted against one of the United States by citizens of another state, or by citizens or subjects of any foreign state.

Article XII

The electors shall meet in their respective states, and vote by ballot for President and Vice President, one of whom, at least, shall not be an inhabitant of the same state with themselves; they shall name in their ballots the person voted for as President, and in distinct ballots the person voted for as Vice President, and they shall make distinct lists of all persons voted for as President, and of all persons voted for as Vice President, and of the number of votes for each, which lists they shall sign and certify, and transmit sealed to the seat of the government of the United States, directed to the President of the Senate;— The President of the Senate shall, in the presence of the Senate and House of Representatives, open all the certificates and the votes shall then be counted;—The person having the greatest number of votes for President, shall be the President, if such number be a majority of the whole number of electors appointed; and if no person have such majority, then from the persons having the highest numbers not exceeding three on the list of those voted for as President, the House of Representatives shall choose immediately, by ballot, the President. But in choosing the President, the votes shall be taken by states, the representation from each state having one vote; a quorum for this purpose shall consist of a member or members from two-thirds of the states, and a majority of all the states shall be necessary to a choice. And if the House of Representatives shall not choose a President whenever the right of choice shall devolve upon them, before the fourth day of March next following, then the Vice President shall act as President, as in the case of the death or other constitutional disability of the President.—The person having the greatest number of votes as Vice President, shall be the Vice President, if such number be a majority of the whole number of electors appointed, and if no person have a majority, then from the two highest numbers on the list, the Senate shall choose the Vice President; a quorum for the purpose shall consist of two-thirds of the whole number of Senators, and a majority of the whole number shall be necessary to a choice. But no person constitutionally ineligible to the office of President shall be eligible to that of Vice President of the United States.

Article XIII

Section 1. Neither slavery nor involuntary servitude, except as a punishment for crime whereof the party shall have been duly convicted, shall exist within the United States, or any place subject to their jurisdiction.

Section 2. Congress shall have power to enforce this article by appropriate legislation.

Article XIV

Section 1. All persons born or naturalized in the United States, and subject to the jurisdiction thereof, are citizens of the United States and of the state wherein they reside. No state shall make or enforce any law which shall abridge the privileges or immunities of citizens of the United States; nor shall any state deprive any person of life, liberty, or property, without due process of law; nor deny to any person within its jurisdiction the equal protection of the laws.

Section 2. Representatives shall be apportioned among the several states according to their respective numbers, counting the whole number of persons in each state, excluding Indians not taxed. But when the right to vote at any election for the choice of electors for President and Vice President of the United States, Representatives in Congress, the executive and judicial officers of a state, or the members of the legislature thereof, is denied to any of the male inhabitants of such state, being twenty-one years of age, and citizens of the United States, or in any way abridged, except for participation in rebellion, or other crime, the basis of representation therein shall be reduced in the proportion which the number of such male citizens shall bear to the whole number of male citizens twenty-one years of age in such state.

Section 3. No person shall be a Senator or Representative in Congress, or elector of President and Vice President, or hold any office, civil or military, under the United States, or under any state, who, having previously taken an oath, as a member of Congress, or as an officer of the United States, or as a member of any state legislature, or as an executive or judicial officer of any state, to support the Constitution of the United States, shall have engaged in insurrection or rebellion against the same, or given aid or comfort to the enemies thereof. But Congress may by a vote of two-thirds of each house, remove such disability.

Section 4. The validity of the public debt of the United States, authorized by law, including debts incurred for payment of pensions and bounties for services in suppressing insurrection or rebellion, shall not be questioned. But neither the United States nor any state shall assume or pay any debt or obligation incurred in aid of insurrection or rebellion against the United States, or any claim for the loss or emancipation of any slave; but all such debts, obligations and claims shall be held illegal and void.

Section 5. The Congress shall have power to enforce, by appropriate legislation, the provisions of this article.

Article XV

Section 1. The right of citizens of the United States to vote shall not be denied or abridged by the United States or by any state on account of race, color, or previous conditions of servitude—

Section 2. The Congress shall have power to enforce this article by appropriate legislation.

Article XVI

The Congress shall have power to lay and collect taxes on incomes, from whatever source derived, without apportionment among the several states, and without regard to any census or enumeration.

Article XVII

Section 1. The Senate of the United States shall be composed of two Senators from each state, elected by the people thereof, for six years; and each Senator shall have one vote. The electors in each state shall have the qualifications requisite for electors of the most numerous branch of the state legislatures.

Section 2. When vacancies happen in the representation of any state in the Senate, the executive authority of such state shall issue writs of election to fill such vacancies: *Provided,* That the legislature of any state may empower the executive thereof to make temporary appointments until the people fill the vacancies by election as the legislature may direct.

Section 3. This amendment shall not be so construed as to affect the election or term of any Senator chosen before it becomes valid as part of the Constitution.

Article XVIII

Section 1. After one year from the ratification of this article the manufacture, sale, or transportation of intoxicating liquors within, the importation thereof into, or the exportation thereof from the United States and all territory subject to the jurisdiction thereof for beverage purposes is hereby prohibited.

Section 2. The Congress and the several states shall have concurrent power to enforce this article by appropriate legislation.

Section 3. This article shall be inoperative unless it shall have been ratified as an amendment to the Constitution by the legislatures of the several states, as provided in the Constitution, within seven years from the date of the submission hereof to the states by the Congress.

Article XIX

Section 1. The right of citizens of the United States to vote shall not be denied or abridged by the United States or by any state on account of sex.

Section 2. Congress shall have power to enforce this article by appropriate legislation.

Article XX

Section 1. The terms of the President and Vice President shall end at noon on the 20th day of January, and the terms of Senators and Representatives at noon on the 3d day of January, of the years in which such terms would have ended if this article had not been ratified; and the terms of their successors shall then begin.

Section 2. The Congress shall assemble at least once in every year, and such meeting shall begin at noon on the 3d day of January, unless they shall by law appoint a different day.

Section 3. If, at the time fixed for the beginning of the term of the President, the President elect shall have died, the Vice President elect shall become President. If a President shall not have been chosen before the time fixed for the beginning of his term, or if the President elect shall have failed to qualify, then the Vice President elect shall act as President until a President shall have qualified; and the Congress may by law provide for the case wherein neither a President elect nor a Vice President elect shall have qualified, declaring who shall then act as President, or the manner in which one who is to act shall be selected, and such person shall act accordingly until a President or Vice President shall have qualified.

Section 4. The Congress may by law provide for the case of the death of any of the persons from whom the House of Representatives may choose a President whenever the right of choice shall have devolved upon them, and for the case of the death of any of the persons from whom the Senate may choose a Vice President whenever the right of choice shall have devolved upon them.

Section 5. Sections 1 and 2 shall take effect on the 15th day of October following the ratification of this article.

Section 6. This article shall be inoperative unless it shall have been ratified as an amendment to the Constitution by the legislatures of three- fourths of the several states within seven years from the date of its submission.

Article XXI

Section 1. The eighteenth article of amendment to the Constitution of the United States is hereby repealed.

Section 2. The transportation or importation into any state, territory, or possession of the United States for delivery or use therein of intoxicating liquors, in violation of the laws thereof, is hereby prohibited.

Section 3. This article shall be inoperative unless it shall have been ratified as an amendment to the Constitution by conventions in the several states, as provided in the Constitution, within seven years from the date of the submission hereof to the states by the Congress.

Article XXII

Section 1. No person shall be elected to the office of the President more than twice, and no person who has held the office of President, or acted as President, for more than two years of a term to which some other person was elected President shall be elected to the office of the President more than once. But this Article shall not apply to any person holding the office of President when this Article was proposed by the Congress, and shall not prevent any person who may be holding the office of President, or acting as President, during the term within which this Article becomes operative from holding the office of President or acting as President during the remainder of such term.

Section 2. This Article shall be inoperative unless it shall have been ratified as an amendment to the Constitution by the legislatures of three fourths of the several states within seven years from the date of its submission to the states by the Congress.

Article XXIII

Section 1. The District constituting the seat of government of the United States shall appoint in such manner as the Congress may direct:

A number of electors of President and Vice President equal to the whole number of Senators and Representatives in Congress to which the District would be entitled if it were a state, but in no event more than the least populous state; they shall be in addition to those appointed by the states, but they shall be considered, for the purposes of the election of President and Vice President, to be electors appointed by a state; and they shall meet in the District and perform such duties as provided by the twelfth article of amendment.

Section 2. The Congress shall have power to enforce this article by appropriate legislation.

Article XXIV

Section 1. The right of citizens of the United States to vote in any primary or other election for President or Vice President, for electors for President or Vice President, or for Senator or Representative in Congress, shall not be denied or abridged by the United States or any State by reason of failure to pay any poll tax or other tax.

Section 2. The Congress shall have power to enforce this article by appropriate legislation.

Article XXV

Section 1. In case of the removal of the President from office or of his death or resignation, the Vice President shall become President.

Section 2. Whenever there is a vacancy in the office of the Vice President, the President shall nominate a Vice President who shall take office upon confirmation by a majority vote of both Houses of Congress.

Section 3. Whenever the President transmits to the President pro tempore of the Senate and the Speaker of the House of Representatives his written declaration that he is unable to discharge the powers and duties of his office, and until he transmits to them a written declaration to the contrary, such powers and duties shall be discharged by the Vice President as Acting President.

Section 4. Whenever the Vice President and a majority of either the principal officers of the executive departments or of such other body as Congress may by law provide, transmit to the President pro tempore of the Senate and the Speaker of the House of Representatives their written declaration that the President is unable to discharge the powers and duties of his office, the Vice President shall immediately assume the power and duties of the office as Acting President.

Thereafter, when the President transmits to the President pro tempore of the Senate and the Speaker of the House of Representatives his written declaration that no inability exists, he shall resume the powers and duties of his office unless the Vice President and a majority of either the principal officers of the executive department or of such other body as Congress may by law provide, transmit within four days to the President pro tempore of the Senate and the Speaker of the House of Representatives their written declaration that the President is unable to discharge the powers and duties of his office. Thereupon Congress shall decide the issue, assemblying within forty-eight hours for that purpose if not in session. If the Congress, within twenty-one days after receipt of the latter written declaration, or, if Congress is not in session, within twenty-one days after Congress is required to assemble, determines by two-thirds vote of both Houses that the President is unable to discharge the powers and duties of his office, the Vice President shall continue to discharge the same as Acting President; otherwise, the President shall resume the powers and duties of his office.

Article XXVI

Section 1. The right of citizens of the United States, who are eighteen years of age or older, to vote shall not be denied or abridged by the United States or by any State on account of age.

Section 2. The Congress shall have power to enforce this article by appropriate legislation.

Article XXVII

No law varying the compensation for the service of Senators and Representatives shall take effect until an election of Representatives shall have intervened.

Meet the Presidents

Up to the present time, there have been 43 presidents of the United States. That is, since the first president, often called "the Father of Our Country," took office in 1789. The term of office of a president is four years, but some presidents have served more than one term, the longest being FDR, or Franklin D. Roosevelt, who was elected for four terms, but served only three. At his death in 1945, Vice President Truman took his place, and then was elected president in his own right.

Here are our presidents. Brief summaries of the events of their administrations follow.

1789–1797 GEORGE WASHINGTON

Offices of Secretary of State, Secretary of Treasury, Postmaster General, and Attorney General set up; Thomas Jefferson as Secretary of State, Alexander Hamilton as Secretary of Treasury, John Jay and James Monroe appointed ambassadors to London and Paris respectively. Congress votes a tariff and excise taxes to pay off federal debt. The Bill of Rights is ratified, the Bank of the United States is set up, public lands are sold to raise funds, a law mandates that the capital would be no further north than the Potomac River. Treaties are signed with England and Spain. In his farewell address, in 1706, President Washington warns against entangling foreign alliances and political party strife.

1798–1801 JOHN ADAMS (Federalist)

Department of Navy set up. Naturalization Act, Alien Act passed by Congress.

1801–1809 THOMAS JEFFERSON (Democratic-Republican)

Supreme Court landmark decision in case of *Marbury v. Madison*, Louisiana Purchase, expansion westward, Lewis and Clark expedition explores Northwest Territory.

1809–1817 JAMES MADISON (Democratic-Republican)

War of 1812 against England, Treaty of Ghent (1815). End of Federalist Party.

1817–1825 JAMES MONROE (Democratic-Republican)

Era of Good Feeling, Monroe Doctrine.

1825–1829 JOHN QUINCY ADAMS (National Republican)

He was the son of the second president. The Erie Canal; New York City becomes important seaport, Noah Webster publishes his *Dictionary*, which became the authority on language, thus helping national unity.

1829–1837 ANDREW JACKSON (Democrat)

Builds the Democratic Party.

1837–1841 MARTIN VAN BUREN (Democrat)

Depression and financial panic. The Panic of 1837, supposedly caused by land speculation and overextension, results in high unemployment and poverty.

1841 WILLIAM HENRY HARRISON

Dies one month after being inaugurated; replaced by the vice president, John Tyler.

1841–1845 JOHN TYLER (Democrat)

First telegraph message sent from Baltimore to Washington. Borders of the country on the North (Canada) and South (Mexico) being discussed.

1845–1849 JAMES K. POLK (Democrat)

Annexation of Texas; Texas enters the Union as a slave state. War breaks out. The Mexican War is a victory for the United States. That, plus the purchase of vast lands in the Southwest from Mexico, makes this a very large country.

1849–1850 ZACHARY TAYLOR (Whig)

California Gold Rush, Forty-niners stampede westward. President dies, to be succeeded by vice president, Millard Fillmore.

1850–1853 MILLARD FILLMORE (Whig)

Compromise of 1850 (admission of free and slave states) prevents the breakup of the Union, *Uncle Tom's Cabin* published.

1853–1857 FRANKLIN PIERCE (Democrat)

Prosperity and peace, but slavery still an important factor in the division of the North and South. Kansas-Nebraska Bill realigns states on issue of slavery; this helps. Japan open to world trade.

1857–1861 JAMES BUCHANAN (Democrat)

Supreme Court landmark decision—*Dred Scott*, Lincoln-Douglas debates, Lincoln wins by a very small margin, and is elected.

1861–1865 ABRAHAM LINCOLN (Republican)

Civil War, Emancipation Proclamation effective January 1, 1863, surrender of Lee in 1865 ends war, Homestead Act, sale of Western land, establishment of land-grant colleges. President assassinated by John Wilkes Booth, April 14, 1865.

1865–1869 ANDREW JOHNSON (Republican)

Reconstruction period; Federal Army sent to the South to keep order; Thirteenth Amendment to the Constitution abolishes slavery forever, Purchase of Alaska, Fourteenth Amendment to the Constitution, equal rights for former slaves, institutes due process of law; civil rights. President impeached by the House of Representatives, tried by the Senate, found not guilty.

1869–1877 ULYSSES S. GRANT (Republican)

Railways extended cross-country, Depression, and Panic, Electoral Commission established. Corruption rampant. Fifteenth Amendment, giving freed men the right to vote, ratified.

1877–1881 RUTHERFORD B. HAYES (Republican)

Elected despite the fact that a Democrat won the popular vote. Prosperity followed by Depression. Indian rebellion put down; Indians forced to live on reservations. Federal army withdrawn from Southern states. Political corruption—the Tweed Ring in New York City (Tammany Hall). Railroad workers strike.

1881 JAMES GARFIELD (Republican)

Assassinated after six months in office, Replaced by vice president, Chester Arthur.

1881–1885 CHESTER ARTHUR (Republican)

Chinese Exclusion Act passed, first Civil Service Reform Bill enacted, rise of Big Business, disputes between labor and management grows.

1885–1889 GROVER CLEVELAND (Democrat)

Civil Service reform extended—pensions. Reduction in tariffs. Union workers riot in Chicago. AFL (American Federation of Labor) formed.

1889–1893 BENJAMIN HARRISON (Republican)

Idaho, Montana, North and South Dakota, Washington (state) and Wyoming admitted to the Union. Sherman Anti-Trust Act passed to control monopolies. Sherman Silver Act passed to permit free coinage of silver with its value fixed at a high level in relation to gold.

1893–1897 GROVER CLEVELAND (Democrat) Second Term

Depression and Panic of 1893 followed by good times and recognition of the United States as a world power. The gold standard and tariff become issues. Hard times for farmers.

1897–1901 WILLIAM McKINLEY (Republican)

Spanish-American War brought on by native rebellion against Spanish rule in Cuba. Treaty of Paris, 1898—Puerto Rico, the Philippines, and Guam become American possessions. Hawaiian Islands annexed. America seen as great naval power. Formation of Pan-American Union. President McKinley reelected for a second term, but six months later, he is assassinated, replaced by the vice president, Theodore Roosevelt.

1901–1909 THEODORE ROOSEVELT (Republican)

Acquisition of the Panama Canal Zone, the result of a revolt by Panama from Colombia. Settlement of Russo-Japanese War. America seen as a great world power. On the domestic scene, a coal miners' strike is settled, Departments of Labor and Commerce established. The "Rough Rider" president, as he was called, is reelected.

1909–1913 WILLIAM HOWARD TAFT (Republican)

Tariff Reform policy defeated. Sixteenth Amendment to the Constitution ratified, establishing an income tax. Antitrust suits against Standard Oil Company and American Tobacco Company instituted.

1913–1921 WOODROW WILSON (Democrat)

Seventeenth Amendment to the Constitution ratified, providing for the direct election of senators. Federal Trade Commission created to prevent unfair competition. Federal Reserve Act regulating banks passed. When war breaks out in Europe, the president declares America to be neutral, but in 1917 diplomatic relations with Germany are broken off over threats of submarine warfare. Congress declares war on April 6, 1917; Amercan troops and supplies are mobilized. Germany signs an armistice on November 11, 1918, ending the war. The Treaty of Versailles signals The League of Nations, the 14 Points for Peace, not adopted. 1919 sees the adoption of the Eighteenth Amendment, women's suffrage, and the Nineteenth Amendment, Prohibition.

1921–1923 WARREN HARDING (Republican)

Period of prosperity and corruption. The president dies in 1923 to be succeeded by the vice president, Calvin Coolidge.

1923–1929 CALVIN COOLIDGE (Republican)

Teapot Dome Scandal. Industrial prosperity, gambling on the stock market rises. The president chooses to not run again.

1929–1933 HERBERT HOOVER (Republican)

Stock market crash, leading to terrible Depression; factories close, banks fail, millions lose jobs, no relief for the needy.

1933–1945 FRANKLIN DELANO ROOSEVELT (Democrat)

The New Deal. Establishment of CCC (Civilian Conservation Corps) and WPA (Works Progress Administration) puts jobless to work. The Social Security Act passed. FDR reelected by large margin. World War II declared, resulting in Selective Service Act, the first peacetime draft in United States. Pearl Harbor, December 7, 1941—The United States declares war on Japan on December 8, and on December 11, Germany and Italy declare war on the United States. Dwight Eisenhower made Supreme Commander of AEF forces. 1944—D-Day, June 6. President, reelected for fourth time, dies April 12, 1945 to be succeeded by vice president, Harry Truman.

1945–1953 HARRY S. TRUMAN (Democrat)

V-E Day, May 6, 1945, victory in Europe. Atomic bombs dropped on Hiroshima and Nagasaki, resulting in end of war. V-J Day, August 15, 1945, victory over Japan. Formation of United Nations at conference in San Francisco. The Marshall Plan for reconstruction of war-damaged locations adopted. Formation of NATO (North Atlantic Treaty Organization). 1950–1951—the Korean War ends in a truce in 1953.

1953–1961 DWIGHT D. EISENHOWER (Republican)

Hawaii and Alaska become states. *Brown v. Board of Education*. Southeast Asia Treaty Organization formed. Space exploration begins, *Sputnik 1* orbits the earth.

1961–1963 JOHN F. KENNEDY (Democrat)

Peace Corps established. Cuban missile crisis. United States guarantees South Vietnam protection from aggression. Nuclear test ban treaty ratified. President assassinated on November 22, 1963, to be succeeded by the vice president, Lyndon Johnson.

1963–1969 LYNDON B. JOHNSON (Democrat)

War on Poverty, the Economic Opportunity Act passed. The war in Vietnam supported with massive military and air aid. Medicare program established. President chooses to not run again.

1969–1974 RICHARD M. NIXON (Republican)

Massive protests against Vietnam war lead to some troops coming home. The president visits China. Astronauts land on the moon. The president is implicated in the Watergate scandal. Televised hearings in the Senate are held regarding a cover-up by the Nixon Administration. Vice President Spiro Agnew resigns; President Nixon appoints Gerald Ford, and his appointment is confirmed by the Senate. Shocking revelations about Watergate are made; the president resigns August 8, 1974, to be succeeded by the vice president, Gerald Ford.

1974–1977 GERALD R. FORD (Republican)

Nixon is granted "full, free and absolute pardon for any crimes he may have committed." President Ford visits South Korea and Japan.

1977–1981 JAMES E. (JIMMY) CARTER (Democrat)

Panama Canal Zone lease terminated. Middle East peace treaties drawn up. SALT II (Strategic Arms Limitation Treaty) negotiated with Russia. In Iran militant students occupy the U.S. embassy and hold 52 Americans hostage. Unsuccessful rescue efforts by the United States are abandoned; eight persons die and the remaining are cruelly treated. Carter is not reelected president, losing the election to Republican Ronald Reagan in a landslide. On the day that the new president is sworn in, January 20, 1981, the hostages are released in Teheran.

1981–1989 RONALD REAGAN (Republican)

Republicans control Senate for the first time in 30 years. First woman appointed to Supreme Court—Sandra Day O'Connor. Budget priorities: sharp increase in defense expenditures with decrease in social programs. 1984 Reagan wins reelection, again by a landslide. Summit meeting with Gorbachev in Geneva. Military aid to Contras in Nicaragua increased by financial help amounting to $100 million. Appointed to Supreme Court: William H. Rehnquist, Chief Justice; Antonin Scalia, Associate Justice. Space shuttle *Challenger*, explodes, killing six astronauts, including first woman. Star Wars program encouraged. Huge trade deficit—a record $169.78 billion.

1989–1993 GEORGE H. W. BUSH (Republican)

Previously vice president to Ronald Reagan, End of Cold War; end of Soviet Union. Noriega overthrown in Panama. Operation Desert Storm successful in the Middle East.

1993–2001 WILLIAM JEFFERSON (BILL) CLINTON (Democrat)

Previously governor of Arkansas. Globalism, peace, and prosperity. Impeached by House of Representatives, but found not guilty when tried by the Senate.

2001– GEORGE W. BUSH (Republican)

Son of President George H. W. Bush. Previously governor of Texas. Terrorist attack on World Trade Center and Pentagon on 9/11/2001. War on Terrorism, Congress appropriates funds to fight. Liberation of Afghanistan from Taliban. War with Iraq—victory, capture of Saddam Hussein.

Immigration Update

I. The Immigration Reform and Control Act of 1986

This law, sometimes referred to as IRCA, took effect in November 1986, when it was signed by President Ronald Reagan. It included the legalization of undocumented aliens (without papers) if they entered the United States before 1982, as well as the legalization of farm workers who worked in the United States between May 1, 1985 and May 1, 1986. If such aliens applied for amnesty (pardon) between May 5, 1987 and May 4, 1988, and established that they

- lived in the United States continuously, without papers, since before January 1, 1982, and can prove such residence, and
- were never found guilty of a crime while here or outside the United States,

they were granted temporary resident status for 18 months. After that they had one year to apply for permanent residence status. But this residence is granted based on the original filing date of the temporary residence application. This results in the five-year waiting period.

More information about eligibility can be obtained by writing to the district offices or the local offices listed in Unit 3. Mark your letter "Attention: Employer Relations Officer, Immigration and Naturalization Service."

II. The Immigration Act of 1990, P.L. 101-649

This law was passed by the 101st Congress and signed into law by President George H. W. Bush on November 29, 1990. Some of its provisions took effect on that date, but those with which we are concerned here, relating to family and job preferences, became effective October 1, 1991. October 14, 1991 was the date of the so-called "green-card lottery" in which the first 40,000 applications from 34 countries qualified for permanent residency.

Provisions of this law include

1. The number of visas for immediate family members has been increased. This applies to citizens, permanent residents, and those who are in the process of establishing residence under the amnesty program. These persons may petition for entry of unmarried sons and daughters, and spouses. Citizens may petition for entry of married sons and married daughters, as well as for their brothers and sisters, provided the latter are at least 21 years old.

2. Workers sponsored by an employer in the United States may be given visas if:
    A. there is a shortage of workers in that line of work;
    B. the worker possesses specialized skills not held by unemployed citizens or legal residents;
    C. the worker has extraordinary ability, or
    D. is an outstanding professor, researcher, or manager;
    E. the applicant is a member of a profession and has an advanced degree;
    F. the worker is skilled and has more than two years' experience, or has graduated from college with a baccalaureate degree;
    G. the worker is unskilled with less than two years' experience. (There is a limit of 10,000 visas per year in this "little skills" class.)

If you have any questions about this law, it would be wise to check with one of the immigrant-serving agencies or an attorney who specializes in immigration law. Other parts of the Immigration Act of 1990 relating to deportation, bonding, antidiscrimination, and so on, while important, have not been included here since they are not directly related to the naturalization process.

Note the new words and phrases used in the text of this law:

spouse	husband or wife
underutilized	not fully used up
minors	children under 21 years of age
immediate relatives	minor children
	parents

III. Highlights of Public Law 104-208—The Illegal Immigration Reform and Immigrant Responsibility Act

This law, signed by President Clinton, became effective on April 1, 1997. Its most important provision prevents readmission to the country by illegal aliens who have left the United States prior to the institution of removal proceedings. There are various ways to obtain relief from the so-called "entitlement bars." This is a long document of more than 300 pages, covering prospective immigration, time limits on requests for asylum, actions on visa overstays, and many relief possibilities. It can be seen in its entirety on the Internet.

IV. Brief Summary of the Child Citizenship Act of 2000

This act, signed by President George W. Bush, amended the INA to facilitate the automatic acquisition of American citizenship for both natural and adopted children of U.S. citizens born outside the United States. If the child is adopted, the adoption must be final. Note that, because of this law, U.S. citizenship will be granted automatically to thousands of children in this country now.

V. Final Regulations on NACARA

The Nicaraguan Adjustment and Central American Relief Act, signed by President Clinton in 1997, provides benefits to certain Central Americans, Cubans, and nationals of former Soviet bloc countries, who came to the United States in the 1980s and 1990s seeking protection here. Legal procedures for establishing the continuity of physical presence/residence here have been released. Such requirements are specifically spelled out. They can be obtained on the Internet by accessing *usdoj.gov*.

Sample Completed Form N-400

When Anneta Quinones received her Application for Naturalization, she began to fill in the answers to the questions. She printed these answers and mailed the completed form, which you will find on the following pages, to the Vermont Service Center, 75 Lower Weldon Street, St. Albans, VT 05479-0001.

As required, she sent two color photographs, taken within the last 30 days, and a copy of her Alien Registration Card. She also sent a money order for $390.

Mrs. Quinones arrived in New York on February 2, 1992 and was eligible for naturalization in 1997, but because of personal problems, did not apply until 2004.

Except for an absence of eight weeks from the United States, Mrs. Quinones has lived continuously in New York State for many years. On Form N-400, she has printed her address for the last five years and has included information about her trip out of the country.

At the present time, Mrs. Quinones is a nurse, but her limited English-speaking skills when she came to this country made it necessary for her to work as a cook in a restaurant for about two years. Information about her job record for the last five years is included in item 6-B. At the present time she has 12 years' experience in a hospital in Brooklyn.

Aurora Quinones, her daughter, is 15 years old and a high school student. She will become a citizen when her mother is naturalized. The law states that a child admitted to the United States of America legally becomes a citizen if either parent is a citizen. Since the child in this case is under 18 years old, she will automatically become a citizen.

OMB No. 1115-0009

Application for Naturalization

Print clearly or type your answers using CAPITAL letters. Failure to print clearly may delay your application. Use black or blue ink.

Part 1. Your Name *(The Person Applying for Naturalization)*

Write your INS "A"- number here:
A 2 1 2 4 1 8 4 1

A. Your current legal name.

Family Name *(Last Name)*

QUINONES

Given Name *(First Name)*

ANNETA

Full Middle Name *(If applicable)*

FOR INS USE ONLY

Bar Code

Date Stamp

B. Your name exactly as it appears on your Permanent Resident Card.

Family Name *(Last Name)*

QUINONES

Given Name *(First Name)*

ANNETA

Full Middle Name *(If applicable)*

Remarks

C. If you have ever used other names, provide them below.

Family Name *(Last Name)*	Given Name *(First Name)*	Middle Name
CABRERA	ANNETA	

D. Name change *(optional)*

Please read the Instructions before you decide whether to change your name.

1. Would you like to legally change your name? ☐ Yes ☐ No
2. If "Yes," print the new name you would like to use. Do not use initials or abbreviations when writing your new name.

Family Name *(Last Name)*

Action

Given Name *(First Name)*

Full Middle Name

Part 2. Information About Your Eligibility   *(Check Only One)*

I am at least 18 years old **AND**

A. ☒ I have been a Lawful Permanent Resident of the United States for at least 5 years.

B. ☐ I have been a Lawful Permanent Resident of the United States for at least 3 years, **AND**
I have been married to and living with the same U.S. citizen for the last 3 years, **AND**
my spouse has been a U.S. citizen for the last 3 years.

C. ☐ I am applying on the basis of qualifying military service.

D. ☐ Other *(Please explain)* _____

Form N-400 (Rev. 07/23/02)N

Figure 21

Part 3. Information About You

Write your INS "A"- number here:
A 2 1 2 4 1 8 4 1

A. Social Security Number
081-05-8153

B. Date of Birth *(Month/Day/Year)*
05 14 1964

C. Date You Became a Permanent Resident *(Month/Day/Year)*
02 02 1992

D. Country of Birth
DOMINICAN REPUBLIC

E. Country of Nationality
DOMINICAN REPUBLIC

F. Are either of your parents U.S. citizens? *(if yes, see Instructions)* ☐ Yes ☒ No

G. What is your current marital status? ☐ Single, Never Married ☐ Married ☐ Divorced ☒ Widowed

☐ Marriage Annulled or Other *(Explain)* _____

H. Are you requesting a waiver of the English and/or U.S. History and Government requirements based on a disability or impairment and attaching a Form N-648 with your application? ☐ Yes ☒ No

I. Are you requesting an accommodation to the naturalization process because of a disability or impairment? *(See Instructions for some examples of accommodations.)* ☐ Yes ☒ No

If you answered "Yes", check the box below that applies:

☐ I am deaf or hearing impaired and need a sign language interpreter who uses the following language: _____

☐ I use a wheelchair.

☐ I am blind or sight impaired.

☐ I will need another type of accommodation. Please explain: _____

_____

_____

Part 4. Addresses and Telephone Numbers

A. Home Address - Street Number and Name *(Do NOT write a P.O. Box in this space)*
1150 MIDWOOD ST.

Apartment Number
3A

City BROOKLYN | **County** KINGS | **State** NY | **ZIP Code** 11225 | **Country** USA

B. Care of

Mailing Address - Street Number and Name *(If different from home address)*

Apartment Number

City | **State** | **ZIP Code** | **Country**

C. Daytime Phone Number *(If any)*
(718) 347-8000

Evening Phone Number *(If any)*
(718) 439-2121

E-mail Address *(If any)*

Form N-400 (Rev. 07/23/02)N Page 2

Figure 21 (cont.)

Write your INS "A"- number here:

A 2 1 2 4 1 8 4 1

Note: The categories below are those required by the FBI. See Instructions for more information.

A. Gender

☐ Male ☒ Female

B. Height

5 Feet 3 Inches

C. Weight

123 Pounds

D. Are you Hispanic or Latino? ☒ Yes ☐ No

E. Race *(Select one or more.)*

☒ White ☐ Asian ☐ Black or African American ☐ American Indian or Alaskan Native ☐ Native Hawaiian or Other Pacific Islander

F. Hair color

☐ Black ☒ Brown ☐ Blonde ☐ Gray ☐ White ☐ Red ☐ Sandy ☐ Bald (No Hair)

G. Eye color

☒ Brown ☐ Blue ☐ Green ☐ Hazel ☐ Gray ☐ Black ☐ Pink ☐ Maroon ☐ Other

A. Where have you lived during the last 5 years? Begin with where you live now and then list every place you lived for the last 5 years. If you need more space, use a separate sheet of paper.

Street Number and Name, Apartment Number, City, State, Zip Code and Country	Dates (Month/Year)	
	From	To
Current Home Address - Same as Part 4.A	01/1994	Present
	__/____	__/____
	__/____	__/____
	__/____	__/____
	__/____	__/____

B. Where have you worked (or, if you were a student, what schools did you attend) during the last 5 years? Include military service. Begin with your current or latest employer and then list every place you have worked or studied for the last 5 years. If you need more space, use a separate sheet of paper.

Employer or School Name	Employer or School Address *(Street, City and State)*	Dates (Month/Year)		Your Occupation
		From	To	
KINGS COUNTY HOSPITAL	CLARKSON AVE. BROOKLYN, NY	01/1994	PRESENT __/____	PRACTICAL NURSE
		__/____	__/____	
		__/____	__/____	
		__/____	__/____	
		__/____	__/____	

Form N-400 (Rev. 07/23/02)N Page 3

Figure 21 (cont.)

Part 7. Time Outside the United States
(Including Trips to Canada, Mexico, and the Caribbean Islands)

Write your INS "A"- number here:
A 2 1 2 4 1 8 4 1 _ _

A. How many total days did you spend outside of the United States during the past 5 years? | 6 1 | days

B. How many trips of 24 hours or more have you taken outside of the United States during the past 5 years? | 1 | trips

C. List below all the trips of 24 hours or more that you have taken outside of the United States since becoming a Lawful Permanent Resident. Begin with your most recent trip. If you need more space, use a separate sheet of paper.

Date You Left the United States (Month/Day/Year)	Date You Returned to the United States (Month/Day/Year)	Did Trip Last 6 Months or More?	Countries to Which You Traveled	Total Days Out of the United States
07101 1999	08130 1 1999	☐ Yes ☒ No	DOMINICAN REPUBLIC	61
__/__/____	__/__/____	☐ Yes ☐ No		
__/__/____	__/__/____	☐ Yes ☐ No		
__/__/____	__/__/____	☐ Yes ☐ No		
__/__/____	__/__/____	☐ Yes ☐ No		
__/__/____	__/__/____	☐ Yes ☐ No		
__/__/____	__/__/____	☐ Yes ☐ No		
__/__/____	__/__/____	☐ Yes ☐ No		
__/__/____	__/__/____	☐ Yes ☐ No		
__/__/____	__/__/____	☐ Yes ☐ No		

Part 8. Information About Your Marital History

A. How many times have you been married (including annulled marriages)? | 1 | If you have NEVER been married, go to Part 9.

B. If you are now married, give the following information about your spouse:

1. Spouse's Family Name *(Last Name)*   Given Name *(First Name)*   Full Middle Name *(If applicable)*

2. Date of Birth *(Month/Day/Year)*   3. Date of Marriage *(Month/Day/Year)*   4. Spouse's Social Security Number

5. Home Address - Street Number and Name   Apartment Number

City   State   ZIP Code

Figure 21 (cont.)

Write your INS "A"- number here:
A 21241841

C. Is your spouse a U.S. citizen? ☐ Yes ☐ No

D. If your spouse is a U.S. citizen, give the following information:

1. When did your spouse become a U.S. citizen? ☐ At Birth ☐ Other

    If "Other," give the following information:

2. Date your spouse became a U.S. citizen

    _ _/_ _/_ _ _ _

3. Place your spouse became a U.S. citizen *(Please see Instructions)*

    City and State

E. If your spouse is NOT a U.S. citizen, give the following information :

1. Spouse's Country of Citizenship

2. Spouse's INS "A"- Number *(If applicable)*

    A _ _ _ _ _ _ _ _ _ _

3. Spouse's Immigration Status

    ☐ Lawful Permanent Resident ☐ Other _____

F. If you were married before, provide the following information about your prior spouse. If you have more than one previous marriage, use a separate sheet of paper to provide the information requested in questions 1-5 below.

1. Prior Spouse's Family Name *(Last Name)*

    QUINONES

Given Name *(First Name)*

    JOSE

Full Middle Name *(If applicable)*

2. Prior Spouse's Immigration Status

    ☐ U.S. Citizen
    ☒ Lawful Permanent Resident
    ☐ Other _____

3. Date of Marriage *(Month/Day/Year)*

    03051989

4. Date Marriage Ended *(Month/Day/Year)*

    09232002

5. How Marriage Ended

    ☐ Divorce ☒ Spouse Died ☐ Other _____

G. How many times has your current spouse been married (including annulled marriages)? ☐

    If your spouse has EVER been married before, give the following information about **your spouse's** prior marriage.
    If your spouse has more than one previous marriage, use a separate sheet of paper to provide the information requested in questions 1 - 5 below.

1. Prior Spouse's Family Name *(Last Name)*

Given Name *(First Name)*

Full Middle Name *(If applicable)*

2. Prior Spouse's Immigration Status

    ☐ U.S. Citizen
    ☐ Lawful Permanent Resident
    ☐ Other _____

3. Date of Marriage *(Month/Day/Year)*

    _ _/_ _/_ _ _ _

4. Date Marriage Ended *(Month/Day/Year)*

    _ _/_ _/_ _ _ _

5. How Marriage Ended

    ☐ Divorce ☐ Spouse Died ☐ Other _____

Form N-400 (Rev. 07/23/02)N Page 5

Figure 21 (cont.)

Write your INS "A"- number here:
A 2 1 2 4 1 8 4 1

A. How many sons and daughters have you had? For more information on which sons and daughters you should include and how to complete this section, see the Instructions.

[1]

B. Provide the following information about all of your sons and daughters. If you need more space, use a separate sheet of paper.

Full Name of Son or Daughter	Date of Birth (Month/Day/Year)	INS "A"- number (if child has one)	Country of Birth	Current Address (Street, City, State & Country)
AURORA QUINONES	04/29/1990 A		DOMINICAN REPUBLIC	1150 MIDWOOD ST. BROOKLYN NY USA
	_ _ / _ / _ _ _ _ A			
	_ _ / _ / _ _ _ _ A			
	_ _ / _ / _ _ _ _ A			
	_ _ / _ / _ _ _ _ A			
	_ _ / _ / _ _ _ _ A			
	_ _ / _ / _ _ _ _ A			
	_ _ / _ / _ _ _ _ A			

Please answer questions 1 through 14. If you answer "Yes" to any of these questions, include a written explanation with this form. Your written explanation should (1) explain why your answer was "Yes," and (2) provide any additional information that helps to explain your answer.

A. General Questions

1. Have you **EVER** claimed to be a U.S. citizen *(in writing or any other way)*? ☐ Yes ☒ No

2. Have you **EVER** registered to vote in any Federal, state, or local election in the United States? ☐ Yes ☒ No

3. Have you **EVER** voted in any Federal, state, or local election in the United States? ☐ Yes ☒ No

4. Since becoming a Lawful Permanent Resident, have you **EVER** failed to file a required Federal, state, or local tax return? ☐ Yes ☒ No

5. Do you owe any Federal, state, or local taxes that are overdue? ☐ Yes ☒ No

6. Do you have any title of nobility in any foreign country? ☐ Yes ☒ No

7. Have you ever been declared legally incompetent or been confined to a mental institution within the last 5 years? ☐ Yes ☒ No

Form N-400 (Rev. 07/23/02)N Page 6

Figure 21 (cont.)

Write your INS "A"- number here:
A 2 1 2 4 1 8 4 1

B. Affiliations

8. a. Have you **EVER** been a member of or associated with any organization, association, fund, foundation, party, club, society, or similar group in the United States or in any other place? ☒ Yes ☐ No

   b. If you answered "Yes," list the name of each group below. If you need more space, attach the names of the other group(s) on a separate sheet of paper.

Name of Group	Name of Group
1. HOSPITAL EMPLOYEES UNION BROOKLYN, NY	6.
2.	7.
3.	8.
4.	9.
5.	10.

9. Have you **EVER** been a member of or in any way associated *(either directly or indirectly)* with:

   a. The Communist Party? ☐ Yes ☒ No

   b. Any other totalitarian party? ☐ Yes ☒ No

   c. A terrorist organization? ☐ Yes ☒ No

10. Have you **EVER** advocated *(either directly or indirectly)* the overthrow of any government by force or violence? ☐ Yes ☒ No

11. Have you **EVER** persecuted *(either directly or indirectly)* any person because of race, religion, national origin, membership in a particular social group, or political opinion? ☐ Yes ☒ No

12. Between March 23, 1933, and May 8, 1945, did you work for or associate in any way *(either directly or indirectly)* with:

    a. The Nazi government of Germany? ☐ Yes ☒ No

    b. Any government in any area (1) occupied by, (2) allied with, or (3) established with the help of the Nazi government of Germany? ☐ Yes ☒ No

    c. Any German, Nazi, or S.S. military unit, paramilitary unit, self-defense unit, vigilante unit, citizen unit, police unit, government agency or office, extermination camp, concentration camp, prisoner of war camp, prison, labor camp, or transit camp? ☐ Yes ☒ No

C. Continuous Residence

Since becoming a Lawful Permanent Resident of the United States:

13. Have you **EVER** called yourself a "nonresident" on a Federal, state, or local tax return? ☐ Yes ☒ No

14. Have you **EVER** failed to file a Federal, state, or local tax return because you considered yourself to be a "nonresident"? ☐ Yes ☒ No

Figure 21 (cont.)

Write your INS "A"- number here:
A 21241841

D. Good Moral Character

For the purposes of this application, you must answer "Yes" to the following questions, if applicable, even if your records were sealed or otherwise cleared or if anyone, including a judge, law enforcement officer, or attorney, told you that you no longer have a record.

15. Have you **EVER** committed a crime or offense for which you were NOT arrested? ☐ Yes ☒ No

16. Have you **EVER** been arrested, cited, or detained by any law enforcement officer (including INS and military officers) for any reason? ☐ Yes ☒ No

17. Have you **EVER** been charged with committing any crime or offense? ☐ Yes ☒ No

18. Have you **EVER** been convicted of a crime or offense? ☐ Yes ☒ No

19. Have you **EVER** been placed in an alternative sentencing or a rehabilitative program (for example: diversion, deferred prosecution, withheld adjudication, deferred adjudication)? ☐ Yes ☒ No

20. Have you **EVER** received a suspended sentence, been placed on probation, or been paroled? ☐ Yes ☒ No

21. Have you **EVER** been in jail or prison? ☐ Yes ☒ No

If you answered "Yes" to any of questions 15 through 21, complete the following table. If you need more space, use a separate sheet of paper to give the same information.

Why were you arrested, cited, detained, or charged?	Date arrested, cited, detained, or charged *(Month/Day/Year)*	Where were you arrested, cited, detained or charged? *(City, State, Country)*	Outcome or disposition of the arrest, citation, detention or charge *(No charges filed, charges dismissed, jail, probation, etc.)*

Answer questions 22 through 33. If you answer "Yes" to any of these questions, attach (1) your written explanation why your answer was "Yes," and (2) any additional information or documentation that helps explain your answer.

22. Have you **EVER**:

a. been a habitual drunkard? ☐ Yes ☒ No

b. been a prostitute, or procured anyone for prostitution? ☐ Yes ☒ No

c. sold or smuggled controlled substances, illegal drugs or narcotics? ☐ Yes ☒ No

d. been married to more than one person at the same time? ☐ Yes ☒ No

e. helped anyone enter or try to enter the United States illegally? ☐ Yes ☒ No

f. gambled illegally or received income from illegal gambling? ☐ Yes ☒ No

g. failed to support your dependents or to pay alimony? ☐ Yes ☒ No

23. Have you **EVER** given false or misleading information to any U.S. government official while applying for any immigration benefit or to prevent deportation, exclusion, or removal? ☐ Yes ☒ No

24. Have you **EVER** lied to any U.S. government official to gain entry or admission into the United States? ☐ Yes ☒ No

Form N-400 (Rev. 07/23/02)N Page 8

Figure 21 (cont.)

E. Removal, Exclusion, and Deportation Proceedings

25. Are removal, exclusion, rescission or deportation proceedings pending against you? ☐ Yes ☒ No

26. Have you **EVER** been removed, excluded, or deported from the United States? ☐ Yes ☒ No

27. Have you **EVER** been ordered to be removed, excluded, or deported from the United States? ☐ Yes ☒ No

28. Have you **EVER** applied for any kind of relief from removal, exclusion, or deportation? ☐ Yes ☒ No

F. Military Service

29. Have you **EVER** served in the U.S. Armed Forces? ☐ Yes ☒ No

30. Have you **EVER** left the United States to avoid being drafted into the U.S. Armed Forces? ☐ Yes ☒ No

31. Have you **EVER** applied for any kind of exemption from military service in the U.S. Armed Forces? ☐ Yes ☒ No

32. Have you **EVER** deserted from the U.S. Armed Forces? ☐ Yes ☒ No

G. Selective Service Registration

33. Are you a male who lived in the United States at any time between your 18th and 26th birthdays in any status except as a lawful nonimmigrant? ☐ Yes ☒ No

If you answered "NO", go on to question 34.

If you answered "YES", provide the information below.

If you answered "YES", but you did NOT register with the Selective Service System and are still under 26 years of age, you must register before you apply for naturalization, so that you can complete the information below:

Date Registered (Month/Day/Year) [   ]   Selective Service Number [_ _ / _ _ _ _ _ _ _ / _]

If you answered "YES", but you did NOT register with the Selective Service and you are now 26 years old or older, attach a statement explaining why you did not register.

H. Oath Requirements *(See Part 14 for the text of the oath)*

Answer questions 34 through 39. If you answer "No" to any of these questions, attach (1) your written explanation why the answer was "No" and (2) any additional information or documentation that helps to explain your answer.

34. Do you support the Constitution and form of government of the United States? ☒ Yes ☐ No

35. Do you understand the full Oath of Allegiance to the United States? ☒ Yes ☐ No

36. Are you willing to take the full Oath of Allegiance to the United States? ☒ Yes ☐ No

37. If the law requires it, are you willing to bear arms on behalf of the United States? ☒ Yes ☐ No

38. If the law requires it, are you willing to perform noncombatant services in the U.S. Armed Forces? ☒ Yes ☐ No

39. If the law requires it, are you willing to perform work of national importance under civilian direction? ☒ Yes ☐ No

Form N-400 (Rev. 07/23/02)N Page 9

Figure 21 (cont.)

Part 11. Your Signature

Write your INS "A"- number here:

A 2 1 2 4 1 8 4 1

I certify, under penalty of perjury under the laws of the United States of America, that this application, and the evidence submitted with it, are all true and correct. I authorize the release of any information which INS needs to determine my eligibility for naturalization.

Your Signature

Anneta Quinones

Date *(Month/Day/Year)*

0 5 2 1 2 0 0 4

Part 12. Signature of Person Who Prepared This Application for You *(if applicable)*

I declare under penalty of perjury that I prepared this application at the request of the above person. The answers provided are based on information of which I have personal knowledge and/or were provided to me by the above named person in response to the *exact questions* contained on this form.

Preparer's Printed Name

Preparer's Signature

Date *(Month/Day/Year)*

_ _ / _ _ / _ _ _ _

Preparer's Firm or Organization Name *(If applicable)*

Preparer's Daytime Phone Number

(   )

Preparer's Address - Street Number and Name

City

State

ZIP Code

Do Not Complete Parts 13 and 14 Until an INS Officer Instructs You To Do So

Part 13. Signature at Interview

I swear (affirm) and certify under penalty of perjury under the laws of the United States of America that I know that the contents of this application for naturalization subscribed by me, including corrections numbered 1 through _____ and the evidence submitted by me numbered pages 1 through _____ , are true and correct to the best of my knowledge and belief.

Subscribed to and sworn to (affirmed) before me _____

Complete Signature of Applicant

Officer's Printed Name or Stamp

Officer's Signature

Date *(Month/Day/Year)*

Part 14. Oath of Allegiance

If your application is approved, you will be scheduled for a public oath ceremony at which time you will be required to take the following oath of allegiance immediately prior to becoming a naturalized citizen. By signing , you acknowledge your willingness and ability to take this oath:

I hereby declare, on oath, that I absolutely and entirely renounce and abjure all allegiance and fidelity to any foreign prince, potentate, state, or sovereignty, of whom or which which I have heretofore been a subject or citizen;

that I will support and defend the Constitution and laws of the United States of America against all enemies, foreign and domestic;

that I will bear true faith and allegiance to the same;

that I will bear arms on behalf of the United States when required by the law;

that I will perform noncombatant service in the Armed Forces of the United States when required by the law;

that I will perform work of national importance under civilian direction when required by the law; and

that I take this obligation freely, without any mental reservation or purpose of evasion; so help me God.

Printed Name of Applicant

Complete Signature of Applicant

Form N-400 (Rev. 07/23/02)N Page 10

Figure 21 (cont.)

Word List

WORD	MEANING
A abbreviation	a shortened form of a word
ability	knowledge and skill needed to do something
abolished	put an end to; did away with
abridge	to make shorter; to lessen
accept	to receive
active	moving; doing one's work, doing things
adjourn	to put off to a later time
administer	to direct or to give
admitted	given the right to enter
adopted	accepted; agreed to; taken as one's own
adult	full-grown; matured
advantage	benefit
advise	inform; tell
afford	to be able to spend money for something
agency	a company or office or organization in business to act for another's benefit
agree	to say "yes"; to have the same opinion
agriculture	the science of farming land
alien	a person from a foreign country; person not yet a citizen
amnesty	a pardon
allegiance	loyalty
allow	to permit
amendment	a change or an addition to a constitution or law
amount	the total sum
annexation	uniting; adding to

WORD	MEANING
anthem	a song or hymn of praise or allegiance
appeal	to take a question from a lower to a higher authority
appeared	was seen; seemed to be
applicant	a person who applies for something
application	a form used to make a request
apply	to ask for something; to let people know you want something
appointed	named to take a job or office
apportion	to make a division
approve	to agree to; to think well of; to say "yes"
area	amount of land; level space
argue	to discuss; give reasons in support of ideas
arrive	to reach a place; come
assemble	to meet together for a common purpose
assistance	help; aid
attorney	a person acting for another person at law
avoid	to keep away from

B

WORD	MEANING
backbone	the most important part
background	the result of training, experience, education
balance	to make equal in value; make even
base	foundation
basic	serving as a starting point
basis	the main part; supporting element
belief	faith; trust
belongings	things a person owns
benefit	anything that is for the good of a person or thing; money paid to a person
bill	a suggested law proposed by a lawmaker
Bill of Rights	the first ten amendments to the Constitution
borrow	to get something from another person with the understanding that it must be returned
boundary	the line, real or imaginary, that shows where a piece of land ends
brief	short

C

WORD	MEANING
cabinet	a group of advisers to the president
candidate	a person who runs for office
capital	the city where the government is located
Capitol	the building in which the U.S. Congress meets
cattle	farm animals; livestock
cause	the thing a person fights for; reason
celebrate	to recognize and honor, as a holiday
census	an official count of people
center	a middle point; place where people meet

WORD	MEANING
certificate	a written statement of proof of some fact
character (good)	a good name or a reputation for being responsible and moral
charge	to ask as a price; fee
cheaper	costing less
check	to control; hold back; restrain
chief executive	the highest officer of government
choice	a thing preferred; selection
choose	to decide to take; pick out
circular	a printed paper containing information
citizen	a person having full rights in the place where he or she lives
civil	relating to private rights; having to do with government service
civil service	government work
claim	to ask for as a right
classified ads	short advertisements listed by alphabet in a newspaper
colonies	settlements in a new land
comfort	something that makes life easier
commerce	trade or business
commissions	small groups of people working for a government
communication	the giving of information
community	a city or town; neighborhood
compare	to show how things are alike or different
compensation	payment for work done or for some other purpose
completes	finishes
comply	obey
concern	anxiety; interest
condition	how a person or thing is
conduct	to manage; carry on
Congress	the main lawmaking body of the United States
conquest	gained by force
consent	to agree; say "yes"
considers	thinks about; makes allowance for
Constitution	the basic law of the United States
contain	to hold; to have; include
continuous	without stopping
contributions	things given to others; gifts
convenience	anything that adds to one's comfort
convention	a meeting for some purpose
conversation	informal talk
costly	expensive; costing a great deal of money
courage	bravery
create	to make

WORD	MEANING
criminal	having to do with a wrongful act against society
crude	rough; not pure
D debate	an argument about issues; to take sides in a discussion
debt	something owed by one person to another or others
decide	to settle a question
declaration	a public statement
Declaration of Independence	a public statement in which the Continental Congress in 1776 said that the 13 colonies were free from Great Britain
Declaration of Intention	a legal paper in which an alien says that he/she intends to become a citizen
declare	to make known openly
defeated	beaten; to win victory over
defense	protection from others
delegate	a person sent to speak or act for others; a representative
democracy	government of, by, and for the people
department	a division or branch of governmental administration
dependent	person needing support—a husband or wife, child, etc.
deposits	material laid down by natural means
deprive	to withhold something from
descendants	children, grandchildren, great-grandchildren
desert	a region without water
destroyed	broken to pieces; ruined; spoiled
difficult	not easy
diploma	a paper that says a person has graduated from a school
disabled	unable to do what most people do; unable to work
disagreement	a difference of opinion; quarrel; dispute
discovered	found
discuss	to talk over
dispute	a heated argument
dissatisfaction	not giving pleasure
dissent	to disagree
district	the part of a state that a congressman represents
document	written proof
domestic	having to do with our own country; relating to household or family
domestic workers	people who do housework for a living
drug	something taken into the body to help a person get well
due process of law	a limit on the actions of government

E

Word	Meaning
earn	to make money by working
education	instruction
effect	(used with "in") operational
elected	chosen by the voters
eligible/eligibility	qualified for something; fit to be chosen
employer	the person or company for whom an individual works
employment	work
energy	power, such as electricity or heat
enforce	make people do something; to compel
enjoy	to like; to have the benefit of something
equality	sameness in importance; being equal
established	started; set up; founded
examination	a test
examiner	a person who examines or questions another person
exception	a situation that doesn't follow the general rule
exciting	giving great joy; stirring one up
executive	the person who runs things; the boss; executive branch of government that enforces law
exist	to live
expensive	costly
experience	what one has done in the past; anything seen, done, or lived through
export	to send to foreign countries
express	say; write; let people know how one feels or thinks
extended	spread; reached out; made longer

F

Word	Meaning
factories	places where things are made
fame	being well known
federation	a group in which members are united but keep self-government
fee	a charge for services or privileges; cost
file	to submit an application or a petition
finally	at the end; at last
fingerprint	the mark of a finger that can be used to identify someone
flows	runs like water
formed	organized; developed; came together
former	the one before; the first
founded	started; built for the first time
freedom	not under control by others; to be able to do as one wants
friendly	kindly
function	a duty or job
furnished	having furniture; put in what was needed

WORD	MEANING
G general	usual; belonging to all
general election	a time when people may vote for any candidate
government	a system of ruling people
graduate	to complete a course of study in a school or college
grant	to give
guarantee	a promise to do something; pledge; stand behind
H hardships	troubles
headed	led by
hemisphere	half of the world
highway	a main road
hires	employs; gives a job to
honor	to show respect
House of Representatives	the lower house of the U.S. Congress
housing project	a group of houses or apartments in one location
I immigrant	a newcomer to a country
immunity	freedom from something
important	meaning much; worthwhile
impress	to make someone remember you; influence
improve	to grow better
include	to form or be a part of something
increase	become larger
independent	free from control by others
individual	a person
industrial centers	places where there are many factories
ineligible	not qualified
informal	not according to rule; without ceremony; relaxed
information	news; knowledge; facts one learns
informed	to know about; to have knowledge of
institution	organization of a public nature
insures	protects; makes certain; guarantees
intelligence	mental power or ability
intelligent	having knowledge; skilled; able to learn quickly
interesting	holds one's attention
interfere	to enter into the affairs of others; meddle; to clash
interpret	to help people to understand
interpreter	a person who explains in one language something that was said in a different language
interview	a conversation between an employer and a person who is asking for a job
invaded	entered with the purpose of taking possession
invented	made for the first time
irrigate	to bring water to crops; to water
issue	a problem needing a decision

J judicial ....having to do with courts and judges and interpreting the laws

jurisdiction ....control

jury ....a group of people sworn to hear the evidence and give a decision in a case

K knowledge ....information; news; facts

L landlord ....a person who owns an apartment house or other rental property

lawfully ....according to the law

lease ....an agreement to rent a house or apartment

legal ....correct according to law; having to do with law

legislation ....making and passing laws

legislative ....having to do with making laws

legislature..the lawmaking body

lending ....allowing the use of something for a while

level..even

librarian ....the person in charge of a library

library ....a building containing a collection of books; also a collection of books

license..to authorize by legal permit

listed..written in order

living..being alive

local...nearby; in one's own neighborhood or city

located ....in; in a certain place

loyal...true to one's friends or country

M majority ....most; more than half of those voting

manufacture ....to make, usually in a factory

marital ....having to do with being married

member...a person who is part of a group of people

mine ....a pit from which coal or ore is dug

minimum ....the smallest number or amount

miracle ....a remarkable thing or event

mode...the way in which something is done

moral...having to do with right and wrong

motor vehicle......................................a car, automobile, or truck

mourned..felt sad

N narrow ....limited; not wide

native-born ....born in the country where a person lives

naturalization hearing.....................an examination of an applicant for citizenship

naturalized ....admitted to citizenship

necessary ....needed; essential

WORD	MEANING
needy	poor; not having enough to live on
neighbor	a person living near another person
neighborhood	a place where people live near one another; community
newcomer	a person in this country for a short time; an alien
nominate	to name or propose for office
nominee	a person named as a candidate for office
notice	to see; a written or printed sign giving information or warning; announcement

O

oath	a solemn promise of the truth of a statement
occupation	the kind of work a person does
official	an officer holding a government job; formal
operate	to work; to act
opinion	a particular judgment or belief; what one thinks
opportunity	a chance to do or get something
ore	rock, sand, or dirt having some metal in it
organize	to get people together for a purpose; plan

P

pamphlet	a little booklet
participate	to take part or share in
pension	regular payment of living expenses to a person who has retired
permanent	steady; lasting; fixed
permit	to allow
persecute	to treat someone cruelly because of his or her beliefs
persecution	cruel treatment of a person because of his or her beliefs
petition	a formal written request
physical	having to do with the body
Pilgrims	settlers who came from England and founded the colony of Plymouth in 1620
Pledge of Allegiance	a formal statement of loyalty to the government
political opinion	a general thought on what is going on in government
politician	a person who works for a political party
politics	affairs of government; management of political affairs
polls	places where people vote
population	people; the number of people in a place
posterity	future generations
postmaster	the person in charge of a post office
poultry	chickens, turkeys, geese, ducks
power	a strong nation; strength; might; force
preamble	the opening part of a statement
precious	dear; of great value

WORD	MEANING
prefer	to like one thing better than another; choose; decide in favor or
prescription	a written order to a druggist telling him or her to make a certain medicine according to a physician's directions
preserve	to keep
prey	to attack; a victim, or one who is helpless under attack
primary election	a time when people nominate, rather than elect, a candidate
principal	main; most important; chief
private	belonging to or concerning an individual; personal; one's own; not public
privately-owned	owned by individuals, rather than a community
privilege	a benefit or advantage
problems	questions
process	a series of actions
proclamation	an official public announcement or notice; official publication
produce	to make or manufacture; grow
products	things made or grown for use
professional	describing a job requiring special education
prohibits	does not permit; forbids
proper	right; correct
protection	providing safety; keeping a person or thing from being harmed
proud	thinking well of oneself
provides	gives; makes possible
public	belonging to the people of a community, state, or nation; not private
public housing projects	a group of houses built by the city, state, or federal government
public office	a position in the service of a nation, state, or city
purposes	reasons for doing something

Q

qualification	a requirement

R

ratify	to approve
reasons	explanations
receipt	a written statement that someone has received something
record	a thing written or kept for future use
references	letters from employers saying how good a worker a person is
refineries	places where raw materials are made ready for use

WORD	MEANING
refugee	a person who leaves a country because of persecution
regarding	about
region	an area; section of a country or state
register	to have one's name written into a list of people who can take a job or can vote
regularly	at certain, expected times
relatives	people in one's own family
religious	relating to faith and worship
remind	to tell again
rent	to pay for the use of land, home, property; the money paid for such use
represent	to speak and work for a person or a group of people
representative	a person chosen to act for another; delegate
republic	a system of representative government
requirement	something needed
residence	a place where a person lives
resource	any supply that will meet a need
respect	to show honor
responsibility	a task; a debt; a duty
retire	to give up a job or office; stop working
right	something to which one has a just claim; any power or privilege given a person by law, custom, etc.
rivals	individuals who are opponents
rule	to guide; govern; control
S sanitation	keeping things clean for health reasons
secret	known only to oneself
security	safety; financial comfort
seeking	looking for
select	to choose
self-educated	taught by oneself
Senate	the upper house of the U.S. Congress
separate	to keep apart; describing things kept apart
separation of powers	duties that have no connection with each other
service	a convenience; a useful thing to be done or given; a helpful act
service trades	jobs that make other people more comfortable
settle	to set up a home; live
share	to use and enjoy together
shortage	too small a number or amount; not enough
shorthand	writing by symbols
skill	great ability
slavery	the owning or keeping of slaves

WORD	MEANING
slogan	a group of words making the purpose of something clear
Social Security	a federal plan to take care of workers in their old age
solved	figured out; found the answer
source	a place where something comes from
specialized	different; unusual; requiring special training
spouse	wife or husband
standard of living	a way of living; things needed and used in order to live in a certain way
"Star-Spangled Banner"	the national anthem of the United States
stationery	articles such as paper, pens, ink, pencils, etc.
stenography	writing in shorthand
strange	not known or heard of before
strength	ability; force; power
structure	a framework, a building
struggle	to battle; fight
suffrage	the right to vote
suggests	hints; mentions
supply	to give, provide, or fill
supreme	highest in importance
surveyor	a person who measures and marks land
survived	lived after others died
sworn	bound by oath
symbol	an object that stands for something else
system of checks and balances	a system in which each branch of government has powers that to some degree control the powers of others

T

WORD	MEANING
tenant	a person who rents an apartment, house, etc. from another person or from a landlord
territory	land; region; land belonging to a government
textiles	woven cloth
trade	business; work one does
trained	taught; made ready and able to do something
traitor	a person who works against his own country
tranquility	the condition of being calm, peaceful, or quiet
treasury	the country's money
treaty	agreement between nations
tuition	money paid to a school in order to attend it
type	kind; sort; to typewrite

U

WORD	MEANING
unalienable	cannot be taken away or lessened
unconstitutional	not according to the Constitution or law
undocumented	without legal documents
uneducated	not trained; unskilled

WORD	MEANING
union	people joined together for a common purpose
unity	being together; being or acting as one
unusual	not common; rare
uphold	to support
urban	relating to a city or town

V

WORD	MEANING
vacancy	an empty apartment, house, or room that can be rented; a job that is open
valid	having force in law
veto	to refuse to allow a bill to become a law by not signing it
vocational	having to do with trades
void	not in force

W

WORD	MEANING
want	to need; something needed
wealth	riches; land; resources; money
welcome	a greeting
wise	to have great understanding of persons, conditions, and situations
witnesses	those who give testimony and evidence
wonder	to think about; want to know why
worship	to pray to; pay honor and respect to

Answer Key

The Flag

PAGE 7

1. Red, white, and blue.
2. Red for courage, white for truth, blue for honor.
3. 13
4. 50
5. "Star-Spangled Banner"

Citizenship

REVIEW   PAGE 10

1–5. See Word List, page 157.
   6. a. Alien.
      b. Easy.
   7. Easy.
   8. A citizen.
   9. Being part of the government of the United States is a benefit of citizenship.
  10. Being able to vote is a citizen's right.

REVIEW   PAGE 12

1–8. See Word List, page 157.
   9. In a U.S. courtroom.
  10. The Oath of Allegiance is a pledge of loyalty to the United States.
  11. To live here and to be part of the country.
  12. Yes.
  13. No.

REVIEW PAGE 13

1. Moving from one place to another.
2. About 40 million.
3. The Immigration Act of 1990.
4. 1899.
5. 1600s.

REVIEW PAGE 15

1-6. See Word List, page 157.
7. The Constitution.
8. 27
9. The Fourteenth Amendment.
10. They are the rights to life, liberty, and property. No matter where I live, these rights cannot be taken away without due process of law.
11. Liberty.

QUIZ PAGE 18

1-7. See Word List, page 157.
8. No.
9. To obey the laws, to know what is going on, to vote, to serve on a jury.
10. To have a voice in government.
11. To make it possible for persons to have a fair trial.
12. To be loyal to the Constitution and government, to obey the laws, to vote, to defend the country, to serve on a jury.

QUIZ PAGE 19

1. You must be at least 18 years old.
2. No.
3. Page 141.
4. Marriage to a citizen.
5. Yes. The USCIS may excuse you from this requirement based on physical or mental disability.

Step 3—Serious Study

PRACTICE TEST PAGE 52

1. Eighteen years old.
2. Yes.
3. You must have resided in this country for five years.* In these five years, you must have been physically present at least 30 months, and you must have resided for at least six months in the state from which you are filing.
4-5. Yes, *unless* you have a physical or developmental disability or a mental impairment that prevents you, or you are over 50 years old and have lived in the United States 20 or more years, or you are over 55 years old and have lived in the United States for 15 or more years.
6. Yes.
7. Yes.
8. Yes.
9. Yes.

---

*A husband or wife of an American citizen may apply for naturalization after three rather than five years' residence, provided that the husband and wife were actually living together during that time.

NOTE: A husband and wife who file for naturalization must do so separately. A husband's naturalization does not make his wife a citizen, or vice versa. Children born abroad may become citizens if they are under 16 years of age at the time their parents are naturalized.

10. Yes. If you have a physical or developmental disability or a mental impairment, you may be exempt from this requirement.

11. The first step in the naturalization process is to obtain an Application for Naturalization (Form N-400) from the Immigration and Naturalization Service. You can get Form N-400 and the other papers that you need by telephoning the INS Forms Line at 1-800-870-3676.

12. It means that you were admitted to this country for permanent residence and that you have a green card.

13. Your name must be spelled exactly as it appears on your Permanent Resident Card so that the records of your lawful admission can be verified. Your address must be exactly right so that you receive promptly any papers mailed to you. Any errors will cause a delay in your becoming a citizen.

14. You may change your name if the judge of the immigration court approves your request.

15. *Employment*—Although immigrants are entitled to work in the United States, they are excluded from holding jobs with the federal government and from some local or state government jobs (those involving peacekeeping).

    Voting—Only citizens can vote.

    Public office—Only citizens can run for public office.

16. A permanent resident.

17. Yes. They are entitled to live here permanently, to travel, to receive most types of public assistance, to work, and to benefit from the full protection of our laws.

18. No. People in the United States with nonimmigrant, or temporary, visas—that is, tourists, students, exchange visitors, and so on—cannot become citizens.

19. No. Although voting is one of the most important benefits of citizenship and every voter must be a citizen, not all citizens exercise this right.

20. Any time after the required residence has been established, usually five years after entering the country for permanent residence or three years for persons married to U.S. citizens.

21. Yes. The Immigration and Naturalization Service has the right to make a neighborhood check or an investigation of the applicant's work site or sites for the five years before filing to determine the character and fitness of the applicant.

22. Yes. Some time after Form N-400 is filed, the applicant will be called to the naturalization interview. There, the naturalization examiner will ask several questions about our government and history.

23. If the applicant is prepared, this examination will be easy. Being prepared means learning as much as you can from this book about government, history, and the meaning of citizenship. It also means finding out about the people who represent you and wanting to make your vote count when you become a citizen.

24. The most important thing to do is to be on time, or a little early, for the appointment. Dress conservatively. In fact, dress as though you were going to a job interview. Bring your Permanent Resident Card. And remember, there is nothing to be nervous about!

25–30. You must look this information up yourself since it pertains to individual matters.

REVIEW PAGE 66

1. Constitution.
2. Ratified.
3. 13
4. Colonies.
5. Americans.
6. They would have to present the idea to a member of Congress who could introduce it as a bill. If it is passed by a two-thirds vote in both houses, it could be sent to the 50 states for ratification. Three-quarters of the state legislatures would have to ratify before it could become part of the Constitution.

REVIEW PAGE 74

1–8. See Word List, page 157.
9. Checks and balances, separation of powers.
10. Legislative, Senate, House of Representatives.
11. Executive.
12. Vice president.
13. Judicial, interprets.

REVIEW PAGE 76

1–6. See Word List, page 157.
7. One represents the 50 states, the other, the people of the state.
8. No.
9. January 3.
10. When members vote to adjourn, or close, the session.
11. Read page 77.
12. The committee system was devised to make the work of Congress easier.

REVIEW PAGE 82

1–9. See Word List, page 157.
10. To carry out the laws.
11. Many responsibilities.

12. The cabinet.
13. No.
14. He takes the Presidential Oath of Office at his inauguration.

REVIEW PAGE 83

1–4. See Word List, page 157.
5. To interpret the laws.
6. Supreme Court.
7. Eight associate justices and one chief justice are all appointed by the president.
8. William Rehnquist.
9. Yes.
10. c
11. c
12. a
13. d

REVIEW PAGE 86

1–8. See Word List, page 157.
9. The Tenth Amendment provides this right.

REVIEW PAGE 91

1–6. See Word List, page 157.
7. Representation.
8. Unalienable.
9. The United States.
10. Traitors, traitor.
11. Dissatisfaction.

REVIEW PAGE 94

1–5. See Word List, page 157.
6. *because* these are the colors of the flag.
7. *because* there were 13 states in the beginning.
8. *because* there are 50 states today.
9. *because* they were part of Britain.
10. *because* the flag was adopted on that date in 1777.

REVIEW   PAGE 95

1. Christopher Columbus, 1492.
2. 1607, Jamestown, Virginia.
3. The Pilgrims.
4. England.
5. Taxes imposed on people who have no voice in the government.
6. July 4, 1776.
7. July 4, 1776.
8. George Washington.
9. Abraham Lincoln was president during the Civil War. He preserved the Union.
10. The Emancipation Proclamation was a document issued by Abraham Lincoln that freed the slaves in the South.
11. A democracy or a republic.
12. The Constitution.
13. 1789.
14. Yes, by amendments, 27 times.
15. Legislative, executive, and judicial.
16. Congress.
17. The Supreme Court.
18. Yes. There are state and local governments.
19. There are 50 states.
20. Red, white, and blue. The red is for courage, the white for truth, and the blue is for honor.
21. The "Star-Spangled Banner."
22. Abraham Lincoln, 1861–1865.
23. It ceases to be in effect.
24. He can veto the bill.
25. Yes, by a two-thirds vote of the Congress.

Appendix   American English Practice

REVIEW   PAGE 111

1. used to
2. have time
3. out of the question
4. lay off
5. a little while
6. write away
7. looking forward
8. heard from
9. Bear in mind
10. breakdown

Basic Requirements for United States Citizenship

Introduction

Many permanent residents choose to apply to become U.S. citizens. The process is called "naturalization." A permanent resident is not required to become a U.S. citizen, but because immigration laws change so often, obtaining citizenship can ensure your ability to live and work freely in the United States. This brief recap will describe the meaning and benefits of citizenship, the requirements for citizenship, the procedure for becoming a citizen, and the ways in which citizenship can be lost.

Definitions and Benefits

A person becomes a U.S. citizen by being born in the United States, by being born abroad to U.S. citizen parents, or by naturalization. All citizens of the United States also are "nationals" of this country, although not all U.S. nationals are U.S. citizens. Generally, U.S. nationals are people who resided in a U.S. territory at the time it was acquired by the United States or who were born in the territory, or born to nationals from the territory, after it was acquired. These days, only American Samoans, Swain Islanders, and residents of the Northern Mariana Islands have the status of noncitizen U.S. nationals.

Naturalization is an administrative process under the jurisdiction of the BCIS. The term "naturalization" means to confer upon a person the rights of a U.S. national. Naturalization confers on you almost all the same rights and benefits as one who is born in the United States possesses. A notable exception is that only natural-born citizens may hold the offices of president and vice president of the United States. A naturalized citizen may hold a seat in the U.S. Congress, but only after having been a naturalized citizen for seven years (for a U.S. representative) or nine years (for a U.S. senator).

A U.S. citizen has the following rights:

- the right to vote
- the right to hold public office (except as just noted)
- the right to engage in any type of employment
- the right to sponsor family members for permanent residence more quickly and easily than permanent residents can. A citizen can sponsor his or her spouse, parent, or child ("immediate relatives") for permanent residence without the immediate relative being subjected to the numerical limits of the country of birth. In addition, the unmarried sons and daughters of citizens are given a higher priority for permanent residence under the numerical limit system.

Perhaps most important, however, is that the BICE cannot remove citizens from the United States, either through deportation or refusal to admit them into the country, unless the BCIS revokes citizenship as discussed below. Major revisions to immigration law have affected—for better or worse—the ability to become or remain a permanent resident. Some of these laws have been retroactive; in other words, some laws take away rights of people who already are permanent residents, even though at the time they became permanent residents, no such laws existed. Therefore, there is much incentive for a permanent resident to become a citizen as soon as he or she is eligible. One possible downside to becoming a citizen is losing the citizenship of your country of birth or of another country of which you have acquired citizenship.

Some states require that, for certain jobs, or to obtain certain licenses, you must be a U.S. citizen or declare your intention to become a citizen. For example, in order to become a certified teacher in the public schools of New York, you must be a citizen or declare your intention to become a citizen. For that reason, the BCIS will allow permanent residents to file forms declaring their intentions to naturalize using Form N-300. You cannot declare your intention to become a U.S. citizen if you are a nonimmigrant, however. Only U.S. permanent residents can make such a declaration, because only permanent residents can apply for citizenship. Nonimmigrants cannot apply for citizenship.

General Requirements for Naturalization

Naturalization is a three-step process:

1. First, you file an application.
2. Second, the BCIS interviews you.
3. Third, you attend a naturalization ceremony at which you take an oath of allegiance and are granted citizenship. You are not a citizen until you have attended the naturalization ceremony and have taken the oath.

You must meet several criteria to be eligible to become a citizen. Some criteria, such as the age requirement, are fairly straightforward. Others, such as whether you have maintained "continuous physical presence," are subject to interpretation. Even if you meet all the criteria, however, you must prove that you are not precluded from becoming a citizen under one of several categories in the law that are designed to keep certain groups of people from becoming citizens.

The BCIS provides an eligibility worksheet and other information with which to determine whether you are eligible for naturalization, as well as study guides and an interactive examination for civics and U.S. government history, on its web site. You can link to the Naturalization Eligibility Worksheet at *http://www.immigration.gov/graphics/services/natz/wsinstruct.htm.*

AGE

You must be at least 18 years old to apply for naturalization. Children under the age of 18 can derive citizenship from their parents.

RESIDENCE

There are several aspects to the residence requirement:

- You must have been lawfully admitted to permanent residence. In other words, if you hold a student visa, visitor visa, or some form of temporary work visa, you are not eligible to apply for citizenship. In addition, you are not eligible for citizenship if the BCIS granted you lawful permanent residence improperly or if you obtained permanent residence by means of willfully misrepresenting material facts.
- You must have been a permanent resident for five years before filing for citizenship (or three years in some cases, as discussed below). The law allows a permanent resident to file a naturalization application up to 90 days *before* reaching that five-year threshold, however.
- The five-year residence must have been continuous.
- You must have been physically present in the United States for at least half of the five-year period.
- For at least three months prior to filing the application, you must have resided in the state or the BCIS district in which you file the application.
- You must reside continuously in the United States from the time the application is filed until the time citizenship is granted.

Where you "reside" is treated by the BCIS in an objective manner. The BCIS looks to where you actually live most of the time, regardless of whether you *intend* some other location to be your residence. The determination of where a person actually and principally resides can be a stumbling block for many people who want to become citizens. For example, if a permanent resident works in the United States but commutes to his or her home in another country (usually Canada or Mexico), he or she cannot satisfy the residency requirements for citizenship until he or she actually makes his or her home and residence here.

The determination of where you reside is related closely to the analysis of whether your residence has been "continuous." For example, the fact that a permanent resident has resided in another country does not mean that person does not *also* reside in the United States. Rather, it means that the person has not resided *continuously* in the United States.

This does *not* mean that it is permissible in all cases for a permanent resident to leave the United States for some lengthy period of time and then return and resume permanent residence. It is important to realize that as a permanent resident, you can abandon your status unless you take steps to preserve it. In fact, if you unwittingly abandon your permanent resident status, you can face deportation on the ground of abandonment once the BCIS discovers, through your naturalization application, that you have left the United States for a long period of time.

Absent abandonment, the fact that you have not resided continuously in the United States for five years prior to filing for naturalization does not endanger your permanent resident status; it means only that you do not meet that requirement of citizenship at the present time. You are not precluded from filing again after you meet the continuous residence requirement.

In addition, the continuous residence requirement pertains only to the five-year period *immediately preceding* the date you file your naturalization application.

You need not be too concerned about losing permanent residence if you take a vacation or otherwise leave the United States briefly, unless you have the intention during that brief time to abandon your permanent resident status. The BCIS *presumes,* however, that an absence of six months or more breaks continuity if it occurs immediately before you filed your application or any time after that up until the date of any denial hearing. You can overcome that presumption by proving that during the absence, you did not intend to, and did not, abandon your U.S. residence. Absences from the United States of more than one year automatically break continuity (except in certain narrow circumstances) whether the absence occurs before or after filing the naturalization application.

PHYSICAL PRESENCE IN THE UNITED STATES

During the required period of continuous residence, you must have been *physically present in the United States* for at least half of the time (that is, 30 months). These 30 months *do not* have to have been continuous but can be calculated by adding up all the time you have spent physically in the United States over the five years prior to filing. This requirement is different from the five-year continuous residence requirement just discussed.

RESIDENCE IN THE STATE OR BCIS DISTRICT

You must reside in the state, or in the BCIS district, in which you will file your application for at least three months immediately before filing. As stated above, the law allows you to file for naturalization up to 90 days prior to five years. If you file 90 days ahead, the BCIS will consider the state residence requirement to be fulfilled if you have resided in the state or BCIS district where the application is filed for three months immediately preceding the BCIS's *examination* of you at the interview.

There are some narrow circumstances in which state residency might be unclear and as to which the BCIS provides guidance.

If you reside in more than one state, you will be deemed to reside in the location in which you file your federal income tax returns.

CONTINUOUS RESIDENCE AFTER FILING

You also must reside continuously in the United States from the date you file your application until the date the BCIS admits you to citizenship. The same rules that apply to absences prior to filing apply to this period of time.

GOOD MORAL CHARACTER

Even though the BICE cannot deport a citizen, the BCIS does apply strict standards of "good moral character" to those who are applying for citizenship. Therefore, the BCIS will perform a background check on you to determine whether you have engaged in any criminal activity. The BCIS will investigate whether you obtained permanent residence lawfully and whether you have become subject to removal since becoming a permanent resident. There are many grounds for removal that also bar a person from being considered to have "good moral character."

Oddly enough, there are many grounds for removal that do not constitute bars to good moral character. For example, a permanent resident who is convicted of a crime of moral turpitude can be removed from the United States, but that same crime, depending on the circumstances, might not prevent the permanent resident from establishing good moral character for naturalization purposes.

Although this might sound like good news on the surface, what it means is that you, as a permanent resident, might unwittingly apply for citizenship only to have the BCIS discover a ground for removal in your application. Rather than finding yourself in a naturalization ceremony, you can find yourself in immigration court in removal proceedings. Therefore, if you ever have been arrested for, or convicted of, any violation or crime, even for a misdemeanor, you should consult an experienced immigration attorney *before* you apply for citizenship, because once you apply you cannot withdraw your application.

The topic of what does and does not constitute "good moral character" could be the subject of an entire book by itself, so this recap provides only a general overview. You *cannot* establish good moral character if, within the five years prior to filing your application, you

- have been convicted of a crime of moral turpitude or of an attempt or conspiracy to commit such a crime
- have been convicted of two or more offenses (whether or not involving moral turpitude) for which the total jail sentence was five years or more

- have been convicted of violating any controlled substance laws
- are or have been an illicit trafficker, or aider/abettor, conspirator, or colluder with others, of prohibited controlled substances or chemicals, except for a single offense of possession of 30 grams or less of marijuana, or are the spouse, son, or daughter of such a person and you have knowingly obtained any financial or other benefit from the person's activity
- have admitted committing the elements of the above crimes (even if you were not convicted)
- have been jailed for a total of 180 days or more because of one or more convictions, no matter when the offenses occurred
- have been convicted of two or more gambling offenses
- have earned your income principally from illegal gambling
- have been engaged in prostitution or commercialized vice
- have been involved in smuggling illegal aliens into the United States (with certain narrow exceptions)
- have been a habitual drunkard
- have practiced, or are practicing, polygamy
- have willfully failed or refused to support your dependents
- have given false testimony under oath in order to receive immigration benefits

Of course, some of these bars to good moral character are subject to interpretation or can be fact-dependent. Even if you are precluded from being found to have good moral character for having committed such acts within the five years prior to your application, at some point in the future you could be eligible to file for citizenship again—if you do not commit similar acts and if the good moral character ground does not involve an offense for which you can be removed.

In addition to these bars for conduct within the five years prior to filing, an applicant is permanently barred from naturalization if he or she ever has been convicted of murder. Further, if he or she has been convicted of an "aggravated felony," as that term is defined in the law, after November 28, 1990, he or she is barred from naturalizing.

Even if you do not fall within one of the categories listed above, the BCIS still can rely on other grounds to find that you do not possess good moral character. The BCIS can evaluate good moral character on a case-by-case basis and can consider conduct that falls outside the specific conduct that legally bars you from being found to have good moral character. This can, but does not automatically, include conduct such as destroying a marriage by an extramarital affair, income tax fraud, and committing unlawful acts that reflect badly on your moral character even if those acts do not bar good moral character automatically.

Generally, the BCIS looks to your conduct during the statutory five-year residence requirement immediately preceding your application to determine good moral character, or the lack of it, but the BCIS is not precluded from looking further back than five years. There are other types of crimes, not listed above, that can be grounds for removal and can prevent naturalization, even if they occurred more than five years immediately prior to filing your application.

As listed above, a person who has given false oral testimony, either in a proceeding or before a BCIS officer or a border patrol agent, in order to obtain an immigration benefit is barred from establishing good moral character. This means, for example, that you can be denied citizenship if you lied on your citizenship application for the purpose of getting citizenship. The law does not make a distinction between "serious" lies and "white" lies when it comes to citizenship applications. Many people who are denied citizenship on this ground have decided not to disclose arrests or convictions on their applications because they believed them to be minor and unimportant and did not want the BCIS know about them. This is a mistake. The BCIS and FBI will conduct a background check. Even if you have been arrested but not charged with anything, there will be a record of the arrest. Answering "no" to the question, "Have you ever been arrested?" is a misrepresentation. Answering "no" to the question, "Have you ever been convicted?" when you have been found guilty of a crime, no matter how petty you believe it to be, is a misrepresentation, even if the record was sealed or expunged. In such cases, the BCIS will not be concerned about how insignificant your conduct was at the time of the arrest; it will concern itself with your failure to be truthful in answering the question on your citizenship application.

Prior immigration violations involving immigration fraud, and conduct involving welfare fraud, also can be grounds for finding that you do not possess good moral character. Gay and lesbian people are not barred from establishing good moral character by virtue of being gay or lesbian.

You must demonstrate good moral character not only for the time preceding your application but throughout processing and right up until the time of your naturalization oath.

ATTACHMENT TO THE PRINCIPLES OF THE U.S. CONSTITUTION

The naturalization application asks questions designed to allow the BCIS examiner to determine whether you will be loyal to the United States. This does not necessarily mean that you have to abandon your country of birth or citizenship unless your country's laws require that you do so.

KNOWLEDGE OF THE ENGLISH LANGUAGE, U.S. HISTORY, AND U.S. GOVERNMENT

You must demonstrate an ability to read, write, and speak words that ordinarily are used in the English language, which amounts to being able to read and write simple words and phrases. The BCIS examiner will test your knowledge of the English language by asking you to write and to speak English. This English test is given at the BCIS naturalization interview using excerpts from the *Federal Textbooks on Citizenship*. If more complex questioning is needed during the interview, interpreters may be used. There are many services available to you if you would like to study for this test. Some resources are listed in this book.

You also must demonstrate knowledge and understanding of the fundamentals of U.S. history and the principles and form of U.S. government. The scope of this examination also is limited to matters covered in the *Federal Textbooks on Citizenship*. This requirement can be satisfied by taking a test at the naturalization interview or by having taken a standardized citizenship test within one year of filing the naturalization application. Only certain tests are acceptable if you are going to take the test ahead of time. In addition, some people who obtained permanent residence under one of the BCIS's special legalization programs might already have fulfilled the history and government tests as part of obtaining legalization.

If you take the test at your interview, the BCIS ordinarily will test your knowledge of U.S. history and government by using a list of 100 standard questions. The number of questions the BCIS examiner asks, and the percentage of questions you will be required to answer correctly, vary from district to district. A list of the 100 most commonly asked questions, and their answers, is reproduced in this book.

You can be excused from the English language, history, and government examinations if you have a "medically determinable" physical or developmental disability or mental impairment that prevents you from meeting those requirements. You can be exempt from the English language examination, but not the history and government examinations, in certain cases involving applicants more than 50 years old.

ABSENCE OF ANY OTHER BAR TO CITIZENSHIP

In addition to the specific requirements for citizenship, there are certain bars to citizenship, which means that under certain circumstances, you might not be eligible for citizenship even if you meet all the specific requirements and even if you are not found to be deportable.

Political Bars

People who are members of, or affiliated with, the Communist party or any other totalitarian party, or who engage in certain advocacy or teaching of such principles, are prohibited from naturalizing. In addition, anarchists, fascists, and people who advocate sabotage are barred, although these terms can be interpreted in various ways. These types of ideological bars to naturalization apply to people who engaged in these activities or advocated these views within ten years prior to filing their naturalization applications.

The association with the political organization must be a "meaningful" one. This clarification is important, because many people (especially young people) join political organizations but do not perform activities other than paying dues, attending meetings, or doing other acts for the organization that do not amount to subversive activity. In addition, in some countries such as the former Soviet Union, children might be required to join political organizations such as Communist youth organizations and might not have a choice in the matter, or adults might be required to join the party to obtain certain jobs. Under circumstances such as those, naturalization will not be barred.

Military Bars

Military-related bars to naturalization include desertion from the military and draft evasion. In certain cases, foreign people who have claimed an exemption from U.S. military service under treaties between their home countries and the United States cannot naturalize. A law passed in 1990 provides, however, that these individuals are not barred from naturalizing if they served in their countries' own military services prior to claiming exemption from U.S. military service.

Criminal Bars

As stated earlier, persons convicted of aggravated felonies after November 28, 1990, are forever barred from naturalizing. In addition, persons who have been convicted of murder at any time cannot naturalize.

Deportation Orders

Most people who are in immigration proceedings or who have final orders of deportation or removal pending against them cannot naturalize.

Incompetence

As stated earlier, persons who are legally incompetent at the time of the naturalization interview or oath of allegiance cannot naturalize.

The BCIS *cannot* preclude you from becoming a U.S. citizen because of your race, gender, or marital status.

SPECIAL CIRCUMSTANCES FOR SPOUSES OF U.S. CITIZENS AND FOR BATTERED SPOUSES AND CHILDREN

Spouses of U.S. Citizens

In addition to fulfilling the requirements set forth above, if you obtained permanent resident status based on marriage to a U.S. citizen, you must provide even more evidence in connection with a naturalization application. There is an advantage to this circumstance, however, in that the five-year residence period discussed above is reduced to three years.

In other words, if you obtained permanent residence based on your marriage to a U.S. citizen, then to be eligible to apply for citizenship, you need only to have been a permanent resident for *three* years, not five years, immediately preceding your application. You can apply up to 90 days in advance of that three-year period (that is, two years and nine months after you obtained permanent resident status). The period of time during which residence must have been continuous is 18 months, not 30 months. Also, the automatic bars to good moral character, discussed earlier, will apply only to those specific types of convictions if they occurred within the three years preceding your application.

Additional evidence burdens are imposed on you, however, if you apply for naturalization and your permanent residence was based on marriage to a U.S. citizen. You must prove that you have lived in "marital union" with your U.S. citizen spouse during the entire three-year residence requirement period. The marital union must have been between you and the same U.S. citizen spouse who originally petitioned for your permanent residence.

Marital union means actually residing together, so divorce, legal separation, and possibly long-term informal separations, terminate the marital union. The law provides that "marital union" must exist for only three years prior to *filing* the naturalization application, not right up until citizenship is granted. The former INS passed a regulation that requires marital union up to the time of the naturalization examination, however. This is contrary to the statute, and a federal court ruled in 1999 that the statute's clear language controls over the INS's regulation. The regulation is still on the books, however, so it is preferable if you can prove marital union throughout the entire naturalization process.

Death of the U.S. citizen spouse terminates marital union. Therefore, your right to naturalize terminates *at any time in the process* upon the death of your U.S. citizen spouse, even if the death occurs after your application has been approved at the interview but *before* you have taken the oath of allegiance.

Another requirement peculiar to these types of cases is that your U.S. citizen spouse must have maintained citizenship during the entire three-year period of continuous residence (in other words, he or she must not have lost citizenship).

Battered Spouses or Children

Another category of persons eligible for the three-year residency period are persons who obtained permanent residence based on their statuses as battered spouses or battered children of U.S. citizens. These spouses and children became subject to the lesser three-year requirement under a new law passed in the year 2000. That same law provides that the battered spouse does not have to prove that he or she lived in marital union with the U.S. citizen for the entire three years, either.

Application Forms, Supporting Documents, and Procedures

As stated earlier, you may apply for naturalization up to three months before the end of your continuous residency requirement. Keep in mind, however, that if you have not had continuous residence or the required physical presence, you might not be eligible to apply that early.

You can find the date that you became a permanent resident by looking at the back of your Alien Registration Receipt Card (green card). The more recent versions of this card, INS Form I-551, have a six-digit number in the first line of numbers on the back of the card. These six numbers represent the year, month, and day of admission to permanent residence. For example, "911016" means October 16, 1991.

Applications for naturalization are filed with BCIS Service Centers, and those Service Centers process the applications and schedule interviews. The BCIS office ultimately in charge of the application will be the office in the BCIS district or state in which you have fulfilled, or will fulfill, the three-month residence requirement. Those offices conduct interviews and make naturalization decisions.

To find the Service Center with which to file your application using your state of residence, go to *http://www.immigration.gov/graphics/fieldoffices/*

index.htm. That site also will show you which district BCIS office will have jurisdiction over your application. There are some exceptions as to where to file your naturalization application, such as when citizenship is based on military service, applications are filed with the BCIS Nebraska Service Center regardless of your residence.

You must file Form N-400, along with evidence of lawful permanent residence, two photographs, and filing and fingerprint fees, with the appropriate BCIS service center. If you believe you are exempt from the naturalization examinations on the basis of disability, you also must file Form N-648. In addition, if you have served in the U.S. armed forces, you must file Form G-325B, a biographical information form, with your application.

The Form N-400 can be filled out from the Internet and printed, or you can print it first and type your answers or print them neatly in ink. It is best to print the form two-sided (page one on one side with page two on the back, etc.). Do not leave any question unanswered. If you need more space to complete an answer, attach a separate sheet of paper that includes your name, a number, and the item number from the form that you are answering.

If the question does not apply to you, write "N/A" (for "not applicable") as the answer to that question. For example, the application at Part 8 asks you to complete information about your current husband or wife. If you have no husband or wife currently, then under "Family name" you would insert "N/A."

There is a difference between the answers "N/A" and "None." If the form requests a specific item, such as other names you have used, and you never have used other names, you should answer "None" to that question.

The questions on Form N-400 appear to be simple, but some can involve complex legal issues. Information provided in the application can lead to removal proceedings, which means that you might lose your permanent resident status on the basis of what you represent in your naturalization application. Many issues that can arise based on the information provided in the form are discussed below. If you even suspect you might have a problem, you should consult an experienced immigration attorney, because you might need help explaining a situation to the BCIS or obtaining a waiver, or you might be advised not to file for naturalization at all.

It is wise to verify that your U.S. Social Security number is valid before submitting your application. Similarly, be sure all documents that record your birth date, such as your birth certificate, passport, and green card, have your correct birth date. Be sure also that all documents that you might be required to submit are valid documents and that they are certified by the appropriate government agency when necessary. The BCIS will investigate the validity of documents, your Social Security number, and other information you provide in your application. At an interview, you can be asked to provide original documents.

The law does not require that you prove your ability to support yourself, or someone else's ability to support you, when applying for naturalization. Therefore, if you are not employed at the time of application or have not been employed over the previous five years, this alone will not prevent you from becoming a citizen (as it could have with permanent residence). Lack of employment might cause the BCIS examiner to question you about your receipt of public benefits, however, and to explore your good faith in obtaining those benefits, which can relate to the "good moral character" requirement for naturalization.

Part 10 of Form N-400 contains 39 questions that pertain to the various grounds for which you potentially can be denied citizenship. If you have any doubt about your answer to any question in this Part, you should consult a qualified immigration attorney. Part 10(B), memberships in organizations, requires

Basic Requirements for United States Citizenship

that you list all the organizations to which you ever have belonged, and not just political organizations but student organizations, social, professional, sports, and other organizations.

Part 10(D) relates to bars to good moral character. The Form N-400 makes it very clear that you are to disclose the requested information no matter when it happened and no matter whether your records are sealed, cleared, or you believe they do not exist. Part 10(D)(15) asks whether you ever have committed a crime or offense for which you have not been arrested. This is a bit of a trick question, because you have to know what the legal elements of a crime or offense are before you can admit having committed it. If you check "yes" to this question, you will be questioned about the conduct, because you can be denied citizenship on good moral character grounds for having committed acts that would have been a basis for a conviction even if you were never arrested, charged, or convicted. If you think you need to answer "yes" to this question, you should consult an experienced immigration attorney. You later will be asked these questions again at your naturalization interview, and you should not answer "I don't know" to this question when the BCIS officer asks you. You should know the answer to this, and all other, questions and be able to back up your answers before you fill out the naturalization application.

The questions in Part 10(D) pertain to criminal and other activity throughout your entire life, not just for the previous three or five years. The instructions under this section are confusing as worded because they imply that you must answer "yes" to these questions. You should answer "yes," however, only if any such question applies to you, and then you must do so regardless of whether an arrest or charge was dismissed or a conviction later was expunged from your records.

Form N-400 includes the question whether you have been "cited" or "detained" by any law enforcement officer for any reason (Part 10(D)(16)). Think carefully about this question before you answer "no" and seek the guidance of an experienced immigration attorney if you have reason to believe you should answer "yes" to this or to any question in Part 10. If you answer "yes" to question G(33) but did not register with the Selective Service System, you have a potential legal problem as well. The willful failure to register for selective service can show lack of good moral character, and conviction for failure to comply with selective service laws is a basis for removal. The questions in Part 10(H) pertain to whether you can be loyal to the United States and are intended to be answered "yes." If you need to answer any of those questions "no," you also should seek legal advice.

You should not fill out Parts 13 and 14, Signature at Interview and Oath of Allegiance, on Form N-400. Rather, at the interview, the BCIS examiner will require you to take an oath and to sign those two parts in front of him or her.

The filing fee for Form N-400 is $320 and a fingerprint fee of $70 must be submitted at the time of filing, for a total of $390 per applicant.

PROCEDURES AFTER FILING

Withdrawals, Amendments, and Transfers

Once you have filed your application for naturalization, you cannot withdraw it without the consent of the BCIS district director. If the district director consents, the BCIS will deny the application but will allow you to apply again in the future. If the district director does not consent to withdrawal, the BCIS will decide your application based on the information you have submitted. If the application is denied, you can appeal.

The application can be amended only to correct clerical errors but not to change any of the information in the application. Therefore, it is important to complete and review your application carefully before you file it. If you move to another BCIS jurisdiction while the application is pending, you can request to have the application transferred to the BCIS office with jurisdiction over the new place of residence. You must make that request by filing Form N-455 with the BCIS office that has jurisdiction over your pending application, and you can make the request up to three months before you move or at any time after you move. The BCIS district director at the office at which the application is pending has discretion to transfer, so a request is not granted automatically. Note that in any case, when you move, you must file Form AR-11 with the BCIS.

Fingerprinting

After you have filed your application, the BCIS will send you a notice that requires you to appear in person at a local BCIS office to have your fingerprints taken. If you cannot appear to be fingerprinted during the period of time set forth in the notice, you must notify the BCIS in writing, provide a reason that you cannot appear during that time, and request that the fingerprint appointment be rescheduled. As with your initial filing, it is wise to send all such correspondence to the BCIS by certified mail with a return receipt requested.

Investigation

While your application is pending and using the fingerprints you provided, the BCIS and the Federal Bureau of Investigation (FBI) will investigate you and your background. The investigation will include a review of the documents and records you have submitted and a review of police records in the United States and other countries.

Additional Documentation

Depending on the outcome of the background investigation, the BCIS might request other documents, such as tax returns, selective service registration letters, divorce certificates, or court dispositions of criminal charges. The BCIS always asks that documents, usually passports and green cards, be taken with you to the interview. Local BCIS offices have their own lists of standard documents required at the interview, and those lists vary.

INTERVIEW

The BCIS will send you a notice that has your interview date in it, along with a list of any documents you are required to take to the interview. Unless serious illness prevents a personal appearance, you must appear at the BCIS office listed in the notice for the naturalization interview. If you receive an interview notice and cannot make it on the date scheduled, you must request in writing to the BCIS that it reschedule your interview. If you fail to attend the interview, the BCIS will close your case but will give you 30 days after the interview date to request that your case be reopened and an interview rescheduled. If you do not make that request to reopen, the BCIS can close your case without deciding it and can give you one year to request reopening. If you do not request reopening within that one-year period, the BCIS will dismiss your application on the ground that you have abandoned it.

The interview will be conducted by an BCIS examiner in English, unless you are exempt from the English language requirement. Even if you are not exempt, if the BCIS examiner believes you meet the basic English language requirements but feels you need an interpreter in order to have a more detailed discussion with you, the BCIS can provide an interpreter. You may have an attorney present with you at the interview.

The BCIS examiner will review Form N-400 with you and make any corrections that might be necessary. If any part of the application is deficient, the BCIS examiner can grant you 60 days to correct the deficiency. The examiner must notify you in writing of what the deficiency is or of what additional evidence must be submitted. Then there will be a reexamination and the BCIS will make a decision. If you have not overcome the deficiency, the BCIS will deny the application.

If you do not pass the English literacy, history, or government test, the BCIS may give you a second chance to take the test(s) within 90 days from your initial interview.

If your application for naturalization is denied for any reason, the BCIS will notify you of the denial and will explain the reason for the denial. The BCIS notice will contain a statement that informs you of your right to an administrative review of the denial.

NATURALIZATION CEREMONY

Even if your application is approved, you are not considered a U.S. citizen until you take the oath of allegiance. You will be required to complete yet another form, BCIS Form N-445, before you take the oath. That forms asks a series of questions designed to update information from the time of your naturalization interview until the time of the ceremony.

Local courts are allowed to choose to have exclusive jurisdiction over administering the oath of allegiance. If a court makes that choice, then only that court can administer the oath to naturalization applicants within its jurisdiction. If your local court has not chosen to have exclusive jurisdiction, then you can choose to take the oath at a court or at a ceremony conducted by the BCIS or an immigration judge. You must make this choice either at the time you apply for naturalization or during your naturalization interview. You must appear in person at the ceremony unless you have a legal excuse.

You will be required to swear in to take the oath or to make a statement that you are taking the oath freely without any reservation or intention to evade the oath. You also will be required to sign the oath. Finally, you will be given a Certificate of Naturalization at the ceremony.

Appealing a Denial

If a BCIS examiner denies your naturalization application, that will be done at the interview stage and you will not proceed to a naturalization ceremony. The BCIS examiner might not make a decision one way or the other at your naturalization interview. By law, however, he or she is supposed to make a decision within 120 days of your interview.

If you wish to appeal the denial, you must proceed first through an administrative appeal to another BCIS officer who has the same rank as or a higher rank than the officer who denied your application. Within 30 days after you receive the denial notice, you must request a review by filing Form N-336 with the local BCIS office that had jurisdiction over your application (*not* with the Service Center where you filed it). You must submit a filing fee of $195 and can submit any other additional evidence, statements, or documents that you believe have a bearing on your case. If you need more time to submit additional evidence, you still must file your appeal notice within 30 days, but along with that notice you can request an extension, in writing, for extra time to file supporting evidence. Your request must include an explanation of a good reason why you need an extension. Whether or not you are seeking more time to file additional evidence, if you fail to file your review request within the 30-day period but file it later, the BCIS will reject your request for review and will not return your filing fee to you.

If you are denied naturalization again after this administrative review, then *and only then* can you ask a federal district court to review your case. In other words, you are required to go through the administrative review first—you cannot go to the court first. You must file your petition for review with the U.S. district court that has jurisdiction over your place of residence. The law provides that you must file the petition no later than 120 days after the BCIS denies your administrative review.

The federal court will conduct what is called a *de novo* review of your naturalization case. This means that the court will make its own decision about your case and will not simply decide whether or not the BCIS was reasonable about the decision it made. You also can ask the court to conduct a hearing, in which evidence can be submitted and witnesses can testify. If the court agrees with you and concludes that the BCIS should not have denied your naturalization application, it can order that the oath of allegiance be administered to you.

There are many possible grounds on which the BCIS can deny naturalization. Denial can be based, for example, on the applicant's failure to pass the history test. Many times, however, the basis for denial of naturalization is that the applicant (a permanent resident) is found to be deportable based on something set forth in the application or through the BCIS's investigation. For example, listing an absence that is lengthy can lead to questions by the BCIS examiner at your interview and then to a request for further evidence, and the examiner might conclude that you have abandoned your permanent residence. If that is the case, you are not eligible to naturalize and, moreover, you no longer are eligible to be a permanent resident. Or, the BCIS's background check could reveal conduct or a conviction that leads the examiner to believe you do not possess "good moral character."

If the application is denied because of deportability, then in addition to denying your application, the BCIS will notify the BICE to institute removal proceedings against you. It is important to understand that you still are entitled to pursue administrative and judicial proceedings to try to have the denial over-turned. Because there was some basis in your application for the denial, how-ever, and because you will have to overcome that basis on appeal, as well as deal with removal proceedings, it is wise to consult an experienced immigration at-torney in this situation. As stated previously, however, if you have any questions or doubts whatsoever you should contact an experienced immigration attorney before you file your application, which could avoid the need for an appeal and prevent possible removal.

Special Rules for U.S. Nationals and Others

Noncitizen nationals are not considered "aliens" and, therefore, they are not subject to immigration laws; that is, they cannot be deported from the United States or refused admission. By the same token, when a territory be-comes independent from the United States, all U.S. nationals from the territory become aliens, whether they reside in the territory or in the United States. A na-tional is entitled to obtain a U.S. passport, and a family-based relative petition filed by a national is treated the same way as a petition filed by a permanent res-ident. A national can apply for naturalization to citizenship under special rules.

A noncitizen national must comply with all the general rules and pro-cedures for naturalization that are discussed above, except the "physical pres-ence" requirement can be fulfilled by physical presence in the outlying U.S. possession rather than in the United States. The national must take up resi-dence in the United States before he or she can naturalize, however, and so must meet the requirement of having resided in the state or BCIS district in which his or her application is filed for at least three months prior to filing.

In addition to filing the forms and evidence discussed earlier, the noncit-izen national must submit a birth certificate or other evidence of national status, proof of identity, and evidence of the three-month state residence requirement.

- Philippine citizens who entered the United States before May 1, 1934 and who resided continuously in the United States since that time were made lawful permanent residents under a 1946 law. Those individuals can naturalize under the standard naturalization procedures.
- Anyone born in Puerto Rico after April 10, 1899 is a U.S. citizen if he or she resided in Puerto Rico, or in any other U.S. territory, on January 13, 1941. People born in Puerto Rico after that date are U.S. citizens at birth.
- Many people who were born in the Virgin Islands (once governed by Denmark) acquired U.S. citizenship by law in 1927. All persons born in the U.S. Virgin Islands after February 24, 1927, are U.S. citizens at birth.

Children of U.S. Citizens

Some children acquire U.S. citizenship automatically at birth. Automatic acquisition of citizenship does not require naturalization. This section deals with the naturalization of children when their U.S. citizen parents apply for them. As stated above, this no longer is done with Form N-400. Rather, the parent files Form N-600, Application for Certificate of Citizenship, on behalf of the child, or the child might derive citizenship automatically under a recent law. This section also deals with the process of deriving citizenship after birth. Therefore, there are three concepts that pertain to children:

1. acquisition of citizenship by birth
2. derivation of citizenship after birth
3. naturalization

"Child" is defined somewhat differently in the naturalization context than in other immigration law contexts. For naturalization purposes, "child" means an unmarried person under 21 years of age. It includes a child who has been legitimated under the law of the child's residence or domicile or under the law of the father's residence or domicile, whether in the United States or elsewhere. A child adopted in the United States also is included in the definition. In cases of legitimation or adoption, however, the legitimation or adoption has to have occurred before the child reached 16 years of age and the child has to have been in the legal custody of the legitimating or adopting parent(s) at the time legitimation or adoption occurred.

The Child Citizenship Act of 2000 radically affects the laws pertaining to derivation of citizenship at birth and naturalization of children by citizen parents. The BCIS currently takes the position that persons who were 18 years of age or older on February 27, 2001, do not qualify for citizenship under that Act. In June 2001, the former INS issued interim regulations pertaining to this new law.

The new law provides that a child born outside of the United States, who is residing in the United States, automatically becomes a U.S. citizen (that is, *derives* U.S. citizenship) when all of the following are met:

- at least one parent is a U.S. citizen, either by birth or by naturalization
- the child is under 18 years of age
- the child is a lawful permanent resident of the United States
- the child resides in the United States in the legal and physical custody of the citizen parent.

The INS did not clarify in its regulations the meaning of the words "residing in" the United States for purposes of this new law. It is reviewing the question, because sometimes children who are living outside the United States still can be considered to be "residing in" the United States for other immigration purposes. Until this issue is resolved, the BCIS and State Department will document a child as a U.S. citizen only in two instances:

- if, on or after February 27, 2001, the child is admitted as a lawful permanent resident and actually is living in the United States (assuming the child is in the legal and physical custody of the U.S. citizen parent)

Basic Requirements for United States Citizenship

- if a child was previously admitted for lawful permanent residence but was absent from the United States on February 27, 2001, the child returned to the United States after February 27, 2001 and was readmitted as a lawful permanent resident (assuming the child is in the legal and physical custody of the U.S. citizen parent)

This will be the practice until a regulation is finalized.

Children who derive citizenship in this way do so automatically. No forms have to be filed. If the parent or child wants documentary proof of citizenship, however, either one can apply to the BCIS for a Certificate of Citizenship (Form N-600, or Form N-643 for adopted children) or can apply to the U.S. Department of State for a U.S. passport.

For children outside the United States who do not fall into the category above, the new law provides that they will acquire citizenship upon approval of a Certificate of Citizenship and taking the oath of allegiance. A Certificate of Citizenship will be issued under the law if all of the following are met:

- at least one parent is a U.S. citizen, either by birth or by naturalization
- the U.S. citizen parent has been physically present in the United States or its outlying possessions for at least five years, at least two of which were after age 14, or the U.S. citizen parent has a citizen parent who has been physically present in the United States or its outlying possessions for at least five years, at least two of which were after age 14
- the child is under 18 years of age
- the child is residing outside the United States in the legal and physical custody of the U.S. citizen parent
- the child is present temporarily in the United States pursuant to a lawful admission and is maintaining lawful status in the United States

These provisions also apply to a child adopted by a U.S. citizen parent if the adoption is finalized before the child's sixteenth birthday and if the child has been in the legal custody of the adopting parent(s) and has resided with them for at least two years, which residence can be either before or after adoption. "Legal custody" of the child means responsibility for and authority over the child.

Different laws about deriving citizenship apply to people who were born at times when other laws controlled. With respect to the Child Citizenship Act of 2000, only children who were under age 18 on February 27, 2001 are eligible to derive citizenship under that law.

Other Grounds for Citizenship

Form N-400, Part 2, Options (C) and (D), describe possible grounds for citizenship other than having fulfilled five or three years in continuous permanent resident status.

Several bars to naturalization deal with military service or evasion of service. Service in the U.S. military also provides some special grounds for naturalization, however. If one of these grounds applies to you, you can check Option (C) of Part 2.

Option (D) of Part 2 requires that you list the section of the law that provides the basis for your naturalization eligibility. Those other grounds are:

- Persons who make extraordinary contributions to U.S. national security
- Spouses of certain U.S. citizens who are stationed abroad in certain positions (residence and physical presence requirements waived)
- Certain employees of U.S. news media organizations (residence and physical presence requirements waived)
- Surviving spouses of U.S. citizens who died during honorable services in active duty in the U.S. military, if living in marital union (residence and physical presence requirements waived)
- Former U.S. citizens who lost their citizenship because they married foreign persons (residence, physical presence, and intent to reside in the United States waived)
- U.S. nationals (discussed earlier) who become residents of any state (U.S. residence and physical presence requirements can be satisfied by residence and presence in the outlying possession)
- U.S. citizens who lost their citizenship because of serving in foreign armies during World War II (must be a permanent resident and intend to reside permanently in the United States, be of good moral character, be attached to the principles of the U.S. Constitution, and take the oath)
- Former U.S. citizens whose nationalities were restored by private legislative bills

Dual Citizenship

If you have dual citizenship, it means that you are a citizen of two countries at the same time. Often one has no control over whether he or she is or can become a dual citizen. Each country has its own citizenship laws, and you are subject to the citizenship law of your country of citizenship as to whether you can retain that country's citizenship upon becoming a U.S. citizen or whether you lose it.

Some countries, such as the United States, allow the children of their citizens to become citizens of their countries at birth, so if you are a permanent resident of the United States and have a child who was born in the United States, that child might be both a U.S. citizen and a citizen of your country of birth or citizenship. Similarly, a U.S. citizen child born in another country might become a citizen of the country of birth under that country's laws.

Under some countries' laws, U.S. citizens might acquire foreign citizenship by marriage to those countries' citizens, or their citizens might lose their native citizenship when they naturalize to U.S. citizenship. U.S. law does not require a person to choose one citizenship or another, so a U.S. citizen who automatically acquires citizenship to another country does not risk losing his or her

Basic Requirements for United States Citizenship

U.S. citizenship. In some cases, however, a U.S. citizen can lose U.S. citizenship by applying for citizenship in another country voluntarily and with the intention of giving up his or her U.S. citizenship.

Most U.S. citizens, including dual citizens, must use a U.S. passport to enter and leave the United States, but if you are a dual citizen you also might be required by the other foreign country of citizenship to use its passport to enter and leave that country. Using your passport from your country of dual citizenship does not endanger your U.S. citizenship.

It is important, then, to learn the rules of your country that are in effect at the time you intend to apply for U.S. citizenship as those laws pertain to your ability to be a dual citizen. If you have to give up your citizenship from another country, you should be clear in your mind that you are willing to do so before you file an application for U.S. citizenship because, as discussed previously, that application cannot be withdrawn once filed.

Acquiring Citizenship at Birth

U.S. citizenship other than that acquired by naturalization is acquired according to place of birth or according to blood relation. Almost everyone who is born in the United States is born a U.S. citizen, but you can be born a U.S. citizen if you are born outside the United States as well. You are a natural-born U.S. citizen if

- you were born in the United States and are subject to its jurisdiction
- you were born in the United States to a member of an Indian, Eskimo, Aleutian, or other aboriginal tribe
- you were born of unknown parentage but were found in the United States while you were under the age of five years, unless or until it is shown prior to your twenty-first birthday that you were not born in the United States
- you were born in Puerto Rico after April 10, 1899 and resided in Puerto Rico, or in any other U.S. territory, on January 13, 1941
- you were born in Puerto Rico after January 13, 1941
- you were born in the U.S. Virgin Islands after February 24, 1927
- you were born in the Canal Zone on or after February 26, 1904, and one or both of your parents, at the time of your birth, was a U.S. citizen
- you were born in the Republic of Panama on or after February 26, 1904 and one or both of your parents, at the time of your birth, was a U.S. citizen employed by the U.S. government or by the Panama Railroad Company or its successor
- you were born in Alaska on or after March 30, 1867, unless you are a noncitizen Indian
- you are an Indian born in Alaska on or after June 2, 1924
- you were born in Hawaii on or after April 30, 1900
- you were born outside the United States and its outlying possessions to U.S. citizen parents, one of whom had a residence in the United States or an outlying possession prior to your birth

- you were born outside of the United States and its outlying possessions to one U.S. citizen parent and one U.S. national parent and the citizen parent was physically present in the United States or a possession for a continuous period of one year prior to your birth
- you were born in a U.S. outlying possession to one U.S. citizen parent who was physically present in the United States or a possession for a continuous period of one year prior to your birth
- you were born outside the United States or its possessions to one alien and one U.S. citizen parent, and the citizen parent, prior to your birth, was physically present in the United States or possession for a total of five years, at least two of which were after age 14 (with some exceptions for government and international organization employees)
- you were born before noon on May 24, 1934, outside U.S. jurisdiction to an alien father and a U.S. citizen mother who had resided in the United States prior to your birth.

You are a U.S. national, but not a U.S. citizen, at birth if

- you were born in a U.S. outlying possession on or after the date of its formal acquisition
- you were born outside the United States and its outlying possessions of parents both of whom are nationals, but not citizens, of the United States and who have had a residence in the United States or one of its outlying possessions prior to your birth
- you were born of unknown parentage but were found in a U.S. outlying possession while you were under the age of five years, unless or until it is shown prior to your twenty-first birthday that you were not born in the outlying possession
- you were born outside the United States and its outlying possessions and one of your parents is an alien and the other a U.S. national (not citizen) who, prior to your birth, was physically present in the United States or its outlying possessions for a total of seven years in any continuous period of ten years, so long as during that time the national parent was not outside the United States or its possessions for a continuous period of more than one year and so long as at least five years were after age 14

Losing Your Citizenship

The U.S. Constitution has been interpreted to provide that the U.S. government cannot take away your citizenship under an "expatriation" law unless you committed acts to give up your citizenship that were intentional and voluntary. That is the case whether you are a citizen by birth or by naturalization. Thus, you can lose your U.S. citizenship:

- by renouncing or relinquishing your citizenship, or
- through denaturalization proceedings initiated by the BICE.

Basic Requirements for United States Citizenship

RENOUNCING OR RELINQUISHING YOUR CITIZENSHIP

Some people have given up (relinquished) their U.S. citizenship in order to avoid certain tax laws and gain tax advantages. If you did this after September 29, 1996, you are subject to a law that provides that you cannot be admitted again to the United States. The Internal Revenue Service (IRS) also imposes penalties for this under current laws.

Immigration law describes seven different actions that natural-born or naturalized U.S. citizens can take to relinquish citizenship. To be found to have relinquished your citizenship, you must have taken one or more of these actions, and you must have done so with the intention of relinquishing your U.S. citizenship. These actions can include serving as an officer in another country's military or formally renouncing your U.S. nationality in front of a U.S. diplomatic or consular officer in another country.

The fact that you might have taken one of these several actions does not alone mean you have lost your citizenship. Rather, the government must prove that loss. In certain cases, if the government proves that you performed one or more of the actions, citizenship loss will be presumed. You then will have the opportunity to prove that you did not perform the action voluntarily (that is, that you did not intend to relinquish your citizenship) and that you did so under duress.

DENATURALIZATION PROCEEDINGS BY THE BICE

The BICE can initiate denaturalization proceedings against naturalized citizens for certain reasons. Through these proceedings, the BICE can revoke citizenship under certain circumstances. For good cause the BICE can institute proceedings in any U.S. district court where a naturalized citizen resides to revoke citizenship and cancel the certificate of naturalization. This can be done on the ground that citizenship was illegally procured or was procured by concealment of a material fact or by willful misrepresentation. If the court revokes citizenship, the revocation is retroactive to the date citizenship was obtained. Fraud, concealment, or misrepresentation must have been intentional on your part and it must have been "material," that is, it must have pertained to some important aspect of your application that led the BCIS to grant your citizenship.

Similarly, if you are convicted of procuring your citizenship, or that of someone else, by fraud, the court automatically will revoke your citizenship. This can include having obtained permanent residence through fraud or willful misrepresentation.

In addition, if a naturalized citizen refuses to testify before a congressional committee about his or her own subversive activities, is convicted of contempt for failing to testify, and continues to refuse to testify within ten years following his or her naturalization, the BICE can consider this a ground for revoking naturalization as having been procured by concealment of a material fact or by willful misrepresentation. Moreover, a person naturalized after December 24, 1952 who, within five years following naturalization, becomes a member of or affiliated with any organization that would have precluded him or her from naturalizing if he or she had been a member at the time, can have naturalization revoked on the ground that he or she was not attached to the principles of the Constitution at the time of naturalization.

Spouses and children who derived citizenship through a person whose citizenship is revoked on the grounds of concealment or misrepresentation also lose their citizenship. If any other ground is the basis for revocation, the spouse and children will not lose citizenship if they reside in the United States at the time of the revocation.

These denaturalization proceedings are brought before courts, not the immigration judges. Only a court can denaturalize a U.S. citizen. *After* your interview but *before* you take the oath of allegiance, however, the BCIS has the power to reopen, modify, or vacate its decision to grant you naturalization.

Internet Resources

United States Government
Nongovernment Agencies and Organizations
Human Rights and Refugee Resources
Immigration Rights Organizations
Foreign Government Embassies
Canadian Immigration Official Web Site

United States Government

Appalachian Regional Commission (ARC) J-1 Waiver Program
http://www.arc.gov/index.do?nodeld=24

Census Bureau
   Home Page   *http://www.census.gov*
   Census Tract Street Locator   *http://censtats.census.gov*
                                  (link to American FactFinder)
   NAICS Codes   *http://censtats.census.gov/cbpnaic/cbpnaic.shtml*
   United States Counties   *http://censtats.census.gov/usa.usa.shtml*

Central Intelligence Agency (CIA)
    Home Page   *http://www.cia.gov*
    World Factbook   *http://www.cia.gov/cia/*
                                           publications/factbook

Department of Agriculture (USDA)
    Home Page   *http://www.usda.gov*
    J-1 Waiver Program: As of February 27, 2002, the USDA
                                           discontinued its J-1 waiver program
                                           abruptly. *See* Chapter 4, J Status.

    Rural-Urban Continuum Codes
                                           http://www.ers.usda.gov/briefing/
                                           rural/data/codes/RUCC.HTM

Department of Commerce
    Home Page   *http://home.doc.gov*
    FedWorld.Gov   *http://www.fedworld.gov*

Department of Health and Human Services
    Home Page   *http://www.hhs.gov*
    Health Professional Shortage Areas (HPSA)
                                           http://bphc.hrsa.gov/databases/
                                           newhpsa/newhpsa.cfm
    Medically Underserved Areas (MUA)/Medically Underserved
        Population (MUP) Database
                                           http://bphc.hrsa.dhhs.gov/
                                           databases/newmua
    Office for Civil Rights   *http://www.hhs.gov/ocr*
    Poverty Guidelines   *http://aspe.os.dhhs.gov/poverty/*
                                           poverty.shtml

Department of Justice
    Home Page   *http://www.usdoj.gov*
    Attorney General   *http://www.usdoj.gov/ag*
    Civil Rights Division   *http://www.usdoj.gov/crt/*
                                           crt-home.html
    Executive Board for Immigration Review
        Home Page   *http://www.usdoj.gov/eoir*
        Board of Immigration Appeals (BIA) Decisions
                                           http://www.usdoj.gov/eoir/efoia/
                                           bia/biaindx.htm
    Office of Chief Administrative Hearing Officer (OCAHO)
                                           http://www.usdoj.gov/eoir/
                                           OcahoMain/ocahosibpage.htm
    Office of Special Counsel for Immigration-Related Unfair
        Employment Practices   *http://www.usdoj.gov/crt/osc*
    Federal Bureau of Investigation (FBI)
                                           http://www.fbi.gov

Department of Homeland Security
Home Page   *http://www.dhs.gov/dhspublic/index/jsp*

Administrative Appeals Unit (AAU)
                                   http://www.immigration.gov/graphics/howdoi/aau.htm

Forms and Fees   *http://www.immigration.gov/graphics/formsfee/forms/index.htm*

BCBP   *http://www.cbp.customs.gov*
BICE   *http://www.bice.immigration.gov./graphics/index.htm*

BCIS On-line   *http://www.immigration.gov/graphics/index.htm*

Color Photo Specifications   *http://www.immigration.gov/graphics/lawsregs/handbook/m-378.pdf*

Detention Standards   *http://www.immigration.gov/graphics/lawsregs/guidance.htm*

Handbook for Employers   *http://www.immigration.gov/graphics/lawsregs/handbook/hand_emp.pdf*

NAFTA Handbook   *http://www.immigration.gov/graphics/sharedlawenfor/bmgmt/inspect/naftahan.pdf*

Naturalization Guide   *http://www.immigration.gov/graphics/services/natz/English.pdf* (available in other languages)

Operations Instructions   *http://www.immigration.gov/lpBin/lpext.dll/inserts/slb/slb-1/slb-44385?f=templates&fn=document-frame.htm#slb-oi*

Information and Privacy   *http://www.immigration.gov/graphics/aboutus/foia/index.htm*

National Central Bureau of INTERPOL
                                   http://www.interpol.int

Department of Labor
Home Page   *http://www.dol.gov*
Bureau of Labor Statistics
Home: *http://stats.bls.gov/home.htm*
Occupational Outlook Handbook
                                   http://www.bls.gov/oco
Standard Occupational Classification (SOC) System
                                   http://stats.bls.gov/soc/home.htm
Dictionary of Occupational Titles (DOT)
                                   http://www.oalj.dol.gov/libdot.htm
Employment Standards Administration (ESA)
                                   http://www.dol.gov/esa/welcome.html
Employment and Training Administration (ETA)
                                   http://www.doleta.gov

Labor Condition Applications (LCAs) Online
> http://workforcesecurity.doleta.gov

Occupational Employment Statistics (OES)
> http://www.bls.gov/oes

Occupational Outlook Handbook (OOH)
> http://www.bls.gov/oco

On-line Wage Library (OWL)   http://edc.dws.state.ut.us/owl.asp
O*Net (Occupational Information)
> http://www.doleta.gov/programs/onet

O*Net Online   http://online.onetcenter.org
Online Forms   http://www.workforcesecurity.doleta.gov/foreign/form.asp

Department of State
Home Page   http://www.state.gov
Affidavit of Support (I-864) http://travel.state.gov/aos.html
Affidavit of Support (FAQs) http://travel.state.gov/i864gen.html
Affidavit of Support Checklist http://travel.state.gov/checklist.html

Bureau of Consular Affairs   http://travel.state.gov
Foreign Affairs Manual   http://foia.state.gov/famdir/Fam/fam.asp

Freedom of Information   http://www.foia.state.gov/aboutfoai.asp

International Information Programs (formerly U.S. Information Agency (USIA))   http://usinfo.state.gov
J Exchange Visitor Program   http://exchanges.state.gov/education/jexchanges

J Exchange Visitor Skills List http://exchanges.state.gov/education/jexchanges/participation/skills/list.pdf

U.S. Embassies/Consulates   http://travel.state.gov/links.html
Visa Bulletin Archives   http://dosfan.lib.uic.edu/erc/visa_bulletin

Visa Bulletins   http://travel.state.gov/visa_bulletin.html

Visa Reciprocity and Country Documents Finder
> http://travel.state.gov/reciprocity/index.htm

Department of the Treasury
Home: http://www.ustreas.gov
U.S. Customs Service: http://www.customs.ustreas.gov

Department of Veterans Affairs
Home Page   http://www.va.gov
Job Vacancies in Health Care http://www.vacareers.com/Search.cfm

FirstGov for Seniors (links to government agencies—not just for seniors!)
> http://www.seniors.gov

Information Agency (USIA) (now is International Information
  Programs—*see* above)   *http://dosfan.lib.uic.edu/usia*

Internal Revenue Service
  Home Page   *http://www.irs.gov*
  Home Page for Individuals   *http://www.irs.gov/individuals/*
                                            index.html
  How to Apply for Taxpayer Identification Number
                                            http://www.irs.gov/pub/irs-pdf/
                                            iw9.pdf
  Form W-7, Application for a Taxpayer Identification Number
    (and other forms)   *http://www.irs.gov/pub/irs-fill/*
                                            fw7.pdf
  IRS Publications (check for periodic updates before relying on these
    publications):
    Publication 54: Tax Guide for U.S. Citizens and Resident
      Aliens Abroad (2002)   *http://www.irs.gov/pub/irs-pdf/*
                                            p54.pdf
    Publication 513: Tax Information for Visitors to the United States
      (December 2001)   *http://www.irs.gov/pub/irs-pdf/*
                                            p513.pdf
    Publication 514: Foreign Tax Credit for Individuals (2002)
                                            http://www.irs.gov/pub/irs-pdf/
                                            p514.pdf
    Publication 515: Withholding of Tax on Nonresident Aliens and
      Foreign Entities (November 2002)
                                            http://www.irs.gov/pub/irs-pdf/
                                            p515.pdf
    Publication 519: U.S. Tax Guide for Aliens (2002)
                                            http://www.irs.gov/pub/irs-pdf/
                                            p519.pdf
    Publication 593: Tax Highlights for U.S. Citizens and
      Residents Going Abroad (August 2000)
                                            http://www.irs.gov/pub/irs-pdf/
                                            p593.pdf
    Publication 597: Information on the U.S.-Canada Income
      Tax Treaty (May 2002)   *http://www.irs.gov/pub/irs-pdf/*
                                            p597.pdf
    Publication 678FS: Volunteer Assistor's Guide - Foreign
      Students (2002)   *http://www.irs.gov/pub/irs-pdf/*
                                            p678fs.pdf
    Publication 686: Certification for Reduced Tax Rates in Tax Treaty
      Countries (December 2001)
                                            http://www.irs.gov/pub/irs-pdf/
                                            p686.pdf
    Publication 901: U.S. Tax Treaties (April 2001)
                                            http://www.irs.gov/pub/irs-pdf/
                                            p901.pdf
    Publication 1915: Understanding Your IRS Individual Taxpayer
      Identification Number (ITIN)
                                            http://www.irs.gov/pub/irs-pdf/
                                            p1915.pdf

Selective Service   *http://www.sss.gov*

Social Security Administration
    Home Page   *http://www.ssa.gov*
    Change of Address   *http://s00dace.ssa.gov/pro/icoa/*
                                 legagreem.shtml
    How to Apply   *http://www.ssa.gov/replace_*
                                 sscard.html
    Form SS-5, Application for a Social Security Card
                                 http://www.ssa.gov/online/ss-5.pdf
    Office Locator   *http://s00dace.ssa.gov/pro/fol/*
                                 fol-home.html

White House   *http://www.whitehouse.gov*

Nongovernment Agencies and Organizations

Commission on Graduates of Foreign Nursing Schools (CGFNS)
                                 http://www.cgfns.org/cgfns/
                                 index.html

Educational Commission for Foreign Medical Graduates (ECFMG)
                                 http://www.ecfmg.org

Federation of State Medical Boards (FSMB)
    Home Page   *http://www.fsmb.org*
    USMLE   *http://www.fsmb.org*
    See also   *http://www.usmle.org*

Fulbright Commissions (Fulbright Association) (Grants)
                                 http://www.fulbright.org/
                                 commissions.htm
    See also   *http://exchanges.state.gov/*
                                 education/fulbright

Institute of International Education (IIE)
                                 http://www.iie.org

National Board of Medical Examiners (NBME)
                                 http://www.nbme.org

United States Medical Licensing Examination (USMLE)
                                 http://www.usmle.org

Human Rights and Refugee Resources

Amnesty International   *http://www.amnesty.org*

Australian Human Rights Page   *http://home.vicnet.net.au/~victorp/
                                                          vphuman.htm*

Center for World Indigenous Studies (CWIS)
                                                          http://www.cwis.org

DIANA Project Sources:
   University of Minnesota Human Rights Library
                                                          http://www1.umn.edu/humanrts
   University of Toronto Bora Laskin Law Library
                                                          *http://www.law-lib.utoronto.ca/
                                                          Diana*
   Yale Law School Human Rights Library
                                                          *http://www.yale.edu/lawweb/
                                                          avalon/diana/index.html*

Forced Migration Projects   *http://www.soros.org/fmp2/
                                                          index.html*

Human Rights Resource Center   *http://www.hrusa.org*

Human Rights Watch   *http://www.hrw.org*

Lawyers Committee for Human Rights
                                                          http://www.lchr.org

Physicians for Human Rights   *http://www.phrusa.org*

United Nations High Commissioner for Refugees (UNHCR)
   Home   *http://www.unhcr.ch/cgi-bin/texis/
                                                          vtx/home*
   Refworld   *http://www.unhcr.ch/research/
                                                          rsd.htm*

United States Department of State Bureau of Democracy, Human
   Rights, and Labor   *http://www.state.gov/g/drl/hr*

Immigration Rights Organizations

American Bar Association (ABA) Immigration Pro Bono Development
  Project   *http://www.abanet.org/*
                                       immigprobono

American Civil Liberties Union (ACLU) - Immigrants' Rights
                                       http://www.aclu.org/issues/
                                       immigrant/hmir.html

National Immigration Forum   *http://www.immigrationforum.org*

NAFSA: Association of International Educators
                                       http://www.nafsa.org

National Network for Immigrant and Refugee Rights (NNIRR)
                                       http://www.nnirr.org

Welfare Information Network (WIN) Immigrants Page
                                       http://www.welfareinfo.org/
                                       immigrant.asp

Foreign Government Embassies

Foreign Embassies in Washington, D.C.
                                       http://www.embassy.org

Foreign Embassies in the United States
                                       http://www.infoplease.com/ipa/
                                       a0004582.html or
                                       http://www.aviso.net/government/
                                       embassies

Canadian Immigration Official Web Site

                                       http://www.cic.gc.ca

Citizenship Study Resources

- The BCIS provides a United States history study guide on its web site at: *http://www.immigration.gov/graphics/services/natz/ushist.pdf.*
- The BCIS provides a United States government study guide on its web site at: *http://www.immigration.gov/graphics/services/natz/usstruct.pdf.*
- English as a Second Language Text. (1989), Government Printing Office Stock No. 027-002-00379-9 (order from Superintendent of Documents, Government Printing Office, Washington, D.C. 20402)
- Sample sentences for written English Test: *http://www.immigration.gov/graphics/services/natzsamp.htm*
- Susan N. Burgess, Esq., *Immigration the Easy Way* (Barron's Educational Series, Inc., 2003)
- There is a fun online self test at: *http://www.immigration.gov/graphics/exec/natz/natztest.asp*

100 Frequently Asked History Questions (and Their Answers)

1. WHAT ARE THE COLORS OF OUR FLAG?

2. HOW MANY STARS ARE THERE IN OUR FLAG?

3. WHAT COLOR ARE THE STARS ON OUR FLAG?

4. WHAT DO THE STARS ON THE FLAG MEAN?

5. HOW MANY STRIPES ARE THERE IN THE FLAG?

6. WHAT COLOR ARE THE STRIPES?

7. WHAT DO THE STRIPES ON THE FLAG MEAN?

8. HOW MANY STATES ARE THERE IN THE UNION?

9. WHAT IS THE 4TH OF JULY?

10. WHAT IS THE DATE, OF INDEPENDENCE DAY?

11. INDEPENDENCE FROM WHOM?

12. WHAT COUNTRY DID WE FIGHT DURING THE REVOLUTIONARY WAR?

13. WHO WAS THE FIRST PRESIDENT OF THE UNITED STATES?

14. WHO IS THE PRESIDENT OF THE UNITED STATES TODAY?

15. WHO IS THE VICE-PRESIDENT OF THE UNITED STATES TODAY?

16. WHO ELECTS THE PRESIDENT OF THE UNITED STATES?

17. WHO BECOMES PRESIDENT OF THE UNITED STATES IF THE PRESIDENT SHOULD DIE?

18. FOR HOW LONG DO WE ELECT THE PRESIDENT?

19. WHAT IS THE CONSTITUTION?

20. CAN THE CONSTITUTION BE CHANGED?

21. WHAT DO WE CALL A CHANGE TO THE CONSTITUTION?

22. HOW MANY CHANGES OR AMENDMENTS ARE THERE TO THE CONSTITUTION?

23. HOW MANY BRANCHES ARE THERE IN OUR GOVERNMENT?

24. WHAT ARE THE THREE BRANCHES OF OUR GOVERNMENT?

25. WHAT IS THE LEGISLATIVE BRANCH OF OUR GOVERNMENT?

26. WHO MAKES THE LAWS IN THE UNITED STATES?

27. WHAT IS CONGRESS?

28. WHAT ARE THE DUTIES OF CONGRESS?

29. WHO ELECTS CONGRESS?

30. HOW MANY SENATORS ARE THERE IN CONGRESS?

31. CAN YOU NAME THE TWO SENATORS FROM YOUR STATE?

32. FOR HOW LONG DO WE ELECT EACH SENATOR?

33. HOW MANY REPRESENTATIVES ARE THERE IN CONGRESS?

34. FOR HOW LONG DO WE ELECT THE REPRESENTATIVES?

35. WHAT IS THE EXECUTIVE BRANCH OF OUR GOVERNMENT?

36. WHAT IS THE JUDICIARY BRANCH OF OUR GOVERNMENT?

37. WHAT ARE THE DUTIES OF THE SUPREME COURT?

38. WHAT IS THE SUPREME LAW OF THE UNITED STATES?

39. WHAT IS THE BILL OF RIGHTS?

40. WHAT IS THE CAPITAL OF YOUR STATE?

41. WHO IS THE CURRENT GOVERNOR OF YOUR STATE?

42. WHO BECOMES PRESIDENT OF THE U.S.A. IF THE PRESIDENT AND THE VICE-PRESIDENT SHOULD DIE?

43. WHO IS THE CHIEF JUSTICE OF THE SUPREME COURT?

44. CAN YOU NAME THE THIRTEEN ORIGINAL STATES?

45. WHO SAID, "GIVE ME LIBERTY OR GIVE ME DEATH"?

46. WHICH COUNTRIES WERE OUR ENEMIES DURING WORLD WAR II?

47. WHAT ARE THE 49TH AND 50TH STATES OF THE UNION?

48. HOW MANY TERMS CAN A PRESIDENT SERVE?

49. WHO WAS MARTIN LUTHER KING, JR.?

50. WHO IS THE HEAD OF YOUR LOCAL GOVERNMENT?

51. ACCORDING TO THE CONSTITUTION, A PERSON MUST MEET CERTAIN REQUIREMENTS IN ORDER TO BE ELIGIBLE TO BECOME PRESIDENT. NAME ONE OF THESE REQUIREMENTS.

52. WHY ARE THERE 100 SENATORS IN THE SENATE?

53. WHO SELECTS THE SUPREME COURT JUSTICES?

54. HOW MANY SUPREME COURT JUSTICES ARE THERE?

55. WHY DID THE PILGRIMS COME TO AMERICA?

56. WHAT IS THE HEAD EXECUTIVE OF A STATE GOVERNMENT CALLED?

57. WHAT IS THE HEAD EXECUTIVE OF A CITY GOVERNMENT CALLED?

58. WHAT HOLIDAY WAS CELEBRATED FOR THE FIRST TIME BY THE AMERICAN COLONISTS?

59. WHO WAS THE MAIN WRITER OF THE DECLARATION OF INDEPENDENCE?

60. WHEN WAS THE DECLARATION OF INDEPENDENCE ADOPTED?

61. WHAT IS THE BASIC BELIEF OF THE DECLARATION OF INDEPENDENCE?

62. WHAT IS THE NATIONAL ANTHEM OF THE UNITED STATES?

63. WHO WROTE THE STAR-SPANGLED BANNER?

64. WHERE DOES FREEDOM OF SPEECH COME FROM?

65. WHAT IS THE MINIMUM VOTING AGE IN THE UNITED STATES?

66. WHO SIGNS BILLS INTO LAW?

67. WHAT IS THE HIGHEST COURT IN THE UNTIED STATES?

68. WHO WAS THE PRESIDENT DURING THE CIVIL WAR?

69. WHAT DID THE EMANCIPATION PROCLAMATION DO?

70. WHAT SPECIAL GROUP ADVISES THE PRESIDENT?

71. WHICH PRESIDENT IS CALLED THE "FATHER OF OUR COUNTRY"?

72. WHAT IMMIGRATION AND NATURALIZATION SERVICE FORM IS USED TO APPLY TO BECOME A NATURALIZED CITIZEN?

73. WHO HELPED THE PILGRIMS IN AMERICA?

74. WHAT IS THE NAME OF THE SHIP THAT BROUGHT THE PILGRIMS TO AMERICA?

75. WHAT WERE THE 13 ORIGINAL STATES OF THE UNITED STATES CALLED?

76. NAME 3 RIGHTS OR FREEDOMS GUARANTEED BY THE BILL OF RIGHTS?

77. WHO HAS THE POWER TO DECLARE WAR?

78. WHAT KIND OF GOVERNMENT DOES THE UNITED STATES HAVE?

79. WHICH PRESIDENT FREED THE SLAVES?

80. IN WHAT YEAR WAS THE CONSTITUTION WRITTEN?

81. WHAT ARE THE FIRST 10 AMENDMENTS TO THE CONSTITUTION CALLED?

82. NAME ONE PURPOSE OF THE UNITED NATIONS.

83. WHERE DOES CONGRESS MEET?

84. WHOSE RIGHTS ARE GUARANTEED BY THE CONSTITUTION AND THE BILL OF RIGHTS?

85. WHAT IS THE INTRODUCTION TO THE CONSTITUTION CALLED?

86. NAME ONE BENEFIT OF BEING A CITIZEN OF THE UNITED STATES.

87. WHAT IS THE MOST IMPORTANT RIGHT GRANTED TO U.S. CITIZENS?

88. WHAT IS THE UNITED STATES CAPITOL?

89. WHAT IS THE WHITE HOUSE?

90. WHERE IS THE WHITE HOUSE LOCATED?

91. WHAT IS THE NAME OF THE PRESIDENT'S OFFICIAL HOME?

92. NAME ONE RIGHT GUARANTEED BY THE FIRST AMENDMENT.

93. WHO IS THE COMMANDER IN CHIEF OF THE U.S. MILITARY?

94. WHICH PRESIDENT WAS THE FIRST COMMANDER IN CHIEF OF THE U.S. MILITARY?

95. IN WHAT MONTH DO WE VOTE FOR THE PRESIDENT?

96. IN WHAT MONTH IS THE NEW PRESIDENT INAUGURATED?

97. HOW MANY TIMES MAY A SENATOR BE RE-ELECTED?

98. HOW MANY TIMES MAY A CONGRESSMAN BE RE-ELECTED?

99. WHAT ARE THE 2 MAJOR POLITICAL PARTIES IN THE U.S. TODAY?

100. HOW MANY STATES ARE THERE IN THE UNITED STATES?

100 Frequently Asked History Questions

1. RED, WHITE, AND BLUE

2. 50

3. WHITE

4. ONE FOR EACH STATE IN THE UNION

5. 13

6. RED AND WHITE

7. THEY REPRESENT THE ORIGINAL 13 STATES

8. 50

9. INDEPENDENCE DAY

10. JULY 4TH

11. ENGLAND

12. ENGLAND

13. GEORGE WASHINGTON

14. GEORGE W. BUSH

15. DICK CHENEY

16. THE ELECTORAL COLLEGE

17. VICE PRESIDENT

18. FOUR YEARS

19. THE SUPREME LAW OF THE LAND

20. YES

21. AMENDMENTS

22. 27

23. 3

24. LEGISLATIVE, EXECUTIVE, AND JUDICIARY

25. CONGRESS

26. CONGRESS

27. THE SENATE AND THE HOUSE OF REPRESENTATIVES

28. TO MAKE LAWS

29. THE PEOPLE

30. 100

31. **(INSERT LOCAL INFORMATION)**

32. 6 YEARS

33. 435

34. 2 YEARS

35. THE PRESIDENT, CABINET, AND DEPARTMENTS UNDER THE CABINET MEMBERS

36. THE SUPREME COURT

37. TO INTERPRET LAWS

38. THE CONSTITUTION

39. THE FIRST 10 AMENDMENTS OF THE CONSTITUTION

40. **(INSERT LOCAL INFORMATION)**

41. **(INSERT LOCAL INFORMATION)**

42. SPEAKER OF THE HOUSE OF REPRESENTATIVES

43. WILLIAM REHNQUIST

44. CONNECTICUT, NEW HAMPSHIRE, NEW YORK, NEW JERSEY, MASSACHUSETTS, PENNSYLVANIA, DELAWARE, VIRGINIA, NORTH CAROLINA, SOUTH CAROLINA, GEORGIA, RHODE ISLAND, AND MARYLAND

45. PATRICK HENRY

46. GERMANY, ITALY, <u>AND</u> JAPAN

47. HAWAII AND ALASKA

48. 2

49. A CIVIL RIGHTS LEADER

50. **(INSERT LOCAL INFORMATION)**

51. MUST BE A NATURAL BORN CITIZEN OF THE UNITED STATES;
MUST BE AT LEAST 35 YEARS OLD BY THE TIME HE/SHE WILL SERVE; MUST HAVE LIVED IN THE UNITED STATES FOR AT LEAST 14 YEARS

52. TWO (2) FROM EACH STATE

53. APPOINTED BY THE PRESIDENT

54. NINE (9)

55. FOR RELIGIOUS FREEDOM

56. GOVERNOR

57. MAYOR

58. THANKSGIVING

59. THOMAS JEFFERSON

60. JULY 4, 1776

61. THAT ALL MEN ARE CREATED EQUAL

62. THE STAR-SPANGLED BANNER

63. FRANCIS SCOTT KEY

64. THE BILL OF RIGHTS

65. EIGHTEEN (18)

66. THE PRESIDENT

67. THE SUPREME COURT

68. ABRAHAM LINCOLN

69. FREED MANY SLAVES

70. THE CABINET

71. GEORGE WASHINGTON

72. FORM N-400, "APPLICATION TO FILE PETITION FOR NATURALIZATION"

73. THE AMERICAN INDIANS (NATIVE AMERICANS)

74. THE MAYFLOWER

75. COLONIES

76. (A) THE RIGHT OF FREEDOM OF SPEECH, PRESS, RELIGION, PEACEABLE ASSEMBLY AND REQUESTING CHANGE OF GOVERNMENT.

(B) THE RIGHT TO BEAR ARMS (THE RIGHT TO HAVE WEAPONS OR OWN A GUN, THOUGH SUBJECT TO CERTAIN REGULATIONS).

(C) THE GOVERNMENT MAY NOT QUARTER, OR HOUSE, SOLDIERS IN THE PEOPLE'S HOMES DURING PEACETIME WITHOUT THE PEOPLE'S CONSENT.

(D) THE GOVERNMENT MAY NOT SEARCH OR TAKE A PERSON'S PROPERTY WITHOUT A WARRANT.

(E) A PERSON MAY NOT BE TRIED TWICE FOR THE SAME CRIME AND DOES NOT HAVE TO TESTIFY AGAINST HIMSELF.

(F) A PERSON CHARGED WITH A CRIME STILL HAS SOME RIGHTS, SUCH AS THE RIGHT TO A TRIAL AND TO HAVE A LAWYER.

(G) THE RIGHT TO TRIAL BY JURY IN MOST CASES.

(H) PROTECTS PEOPLE AGAINST EXCESSIVE OR UNREASONABLE FINES OR CRUEL AND UNUSUAL PUNISHMENT.

(I) THE PEOPLE HAVE RIGHTS OTHER THAN THOSE MENTIONED IN THE CONSTITUTION. ANY POWER NOT GIVEN TO THE FEDERAL GOVERNMENT BY THE CONSTITUTION IS A POWER OF EITHER THE STATE OR THE PEOPLE.

77. THE CONGRESS

78. REPUBLICAN

79. ABRAHAM LINCOLN

80. 1787

81. THE BILL OF RIGHTS

82. FOR COUNTRIES TO DISCUSS AND TRY TO RESOLVE WORLD PROBLEMS; TO PROVIDE ECONOMIC AID TO MANY COUNTRIES.

83. IN THE CAPITOL IN WASHINGTON, D.C.

84. EVERYONE (CITIZENS AND NON-CITIZENS LIVING IN THE U.S.)

85. THE PREAMBLE

86. OBTAIN FEDERAL GOVERNMENT JOBS; TRAVEL WITH A U.S. PASSPORT; PETITION FOR CLOSE RELATIVES TO COME TO THE U.S. TO LIVE

87. THE RIGHT TO VOTE

88. THE PLACE WHERE CONGRESS MEETS

89. THE PRESIDENT'S OFFICIAL HOME

90. WASHINGTON, D.C. (1600 PENNSYLVANIA AVENUE, NW)

91. THE WHITE HOUSE

92. FREEDOM OF: SPEECH, PRESS, RELIGION, PEACEABLE ASSEMBLY, AND REQUESTING CHANGE OF THE GOVERNMENT

93. THE PRESIDENT

94.   GEORGE WASHINGTON

95.   NOVEMBER

96.   JANUARY

97.   THERE IS NO LIMIT

98.   THERE IS NO LIMIT

99.   DEMOCRATIC AND REPUBLICAN

100.   (50)

Index

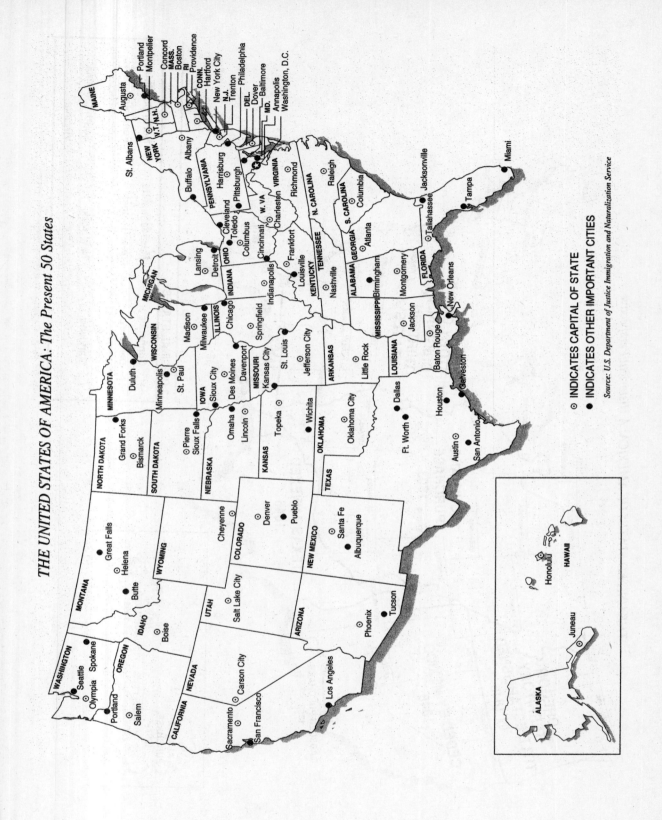

THE UNITED STATES OF AMERICA: The Present 50 States

⊙ INDICATES CAPITAL OF STATE

● INDICATES OTHER IMPORTANT CITIES

Source: U.S. Department of Justice Immigration and Naturalization Service

THE UNITED STATES OF AMERICA: A Historical Perspective

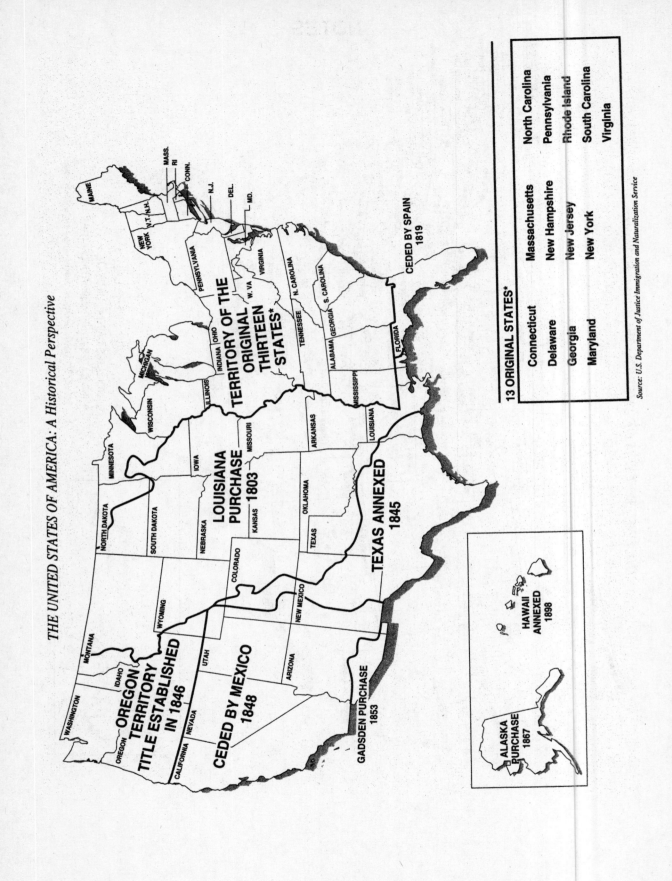

13 ORIGINAL STATES*

Connecticut	Massachusetts	North Carolina
Delaware	New Hampshire	Pennsylvania
Georgia	New Jersey	Rhode Island
Maryland	New York	South Carolina
		Virginia

Source: U.S. Department of Justice Immigration and Naturalization Service

NOTES

NOTES

NOTES

NOTES

NOTES

NOTES